More Praise for *Karmic Choices*

"There can be no higher calling for the human being than to understand the totality of who we are. This book is a key to that knowledge, which becomes wisdom when we apply the karmic choices that Wojton presents so clearly for us to see."
—Alan Steinfeld, founder of NewRealities.com

"Djuna is one of the spiritual community's most beautiful, compassionate, caring, collaborative, and incisive beings … [I] recommend her new book, *Karmic Choices,* to anyone with a sincere desire to grow, to learn, and to experience their ultimate destiny."
—Allan Silberhartz, host of Bridging Heaven and Earth International Television Format for Awakening

"Our sister Djuna is a person of great spiritual and personal qualities who studies the Shipibo medicine tradition at our school here in the Amazon jungle of Ucayali, Peru … She is someone who sees the value in our medicine's power to heal people, and share its merits with her people."
—Pedro Tangoa-Chonon Rawa, *Presidente de la Escuela Universal Ancestral de Merrayas Shipibo-Conibo de la Amazonia Peruana*

"Djuna Wojton helps the reader connect with their authentic self and in the process release profound fears, hurts, anger, shame and guilt and increase their joy, love, peace

D1359778

and love … this book [is] an excellent, practical manual for personal, relationship, and spiritual growth."

—Philip H. Friedman, PhD, licensed psychologist, director of the Foundation for Well-Being (Philadelphia Area), and author of *The Forgiveness Solution*

"Djuna's the real deal! Not only has she been a pioneer of New Thought, she is a gifted and wise healer with a long-standing practice … Her inspiring writing rests on a foundation of real world experience and she's got a proven track record for touching hearts deeply."

—Joni Carly, co-author with Deepak Chopra, Jack Canfield, and Dr. Denis Waitley of *Stepping Stones to Success*

KARMIC CHOICES

About the Author

Djuna Wojton is a spiritual healer, tarot reader, and astrologer with over two decades of experience. She is the director of the Djunaverse Center for Healing Arts in Philadelphia, which helps clients from around the world through classes and private sessions that focus on personal growth. She also writes weekly and monthly astrology columns, produces weekly video forecasts for Oranum.com and documentary films for her healing arts channel on http://www.youtube.com/user/DjunaWojton, blogs on djunaverse.com, and contributes articles to newrealities.com. She is the author of *Karmic Healing: Clearing Past-Life Blocks to Present-Day Love, Health, and Happiness.*

DJUNA WOJTON

KARMIC CHOICES

HOW MAKING THE RIGHT
DECISIONS CAN CREATE
ENDURING JOY

Llewellyn Publications
Woodbury, Minnesota

Karmic Choices: How Making the Right Decisions Can Create Enduring Joy ©
2014 by Djuna Wojton. All rights reserved. No part of this book may be used or
reproduced in any manner whatsoever, including Internet usage, without written
permission from Llewellyn Publications, except in the case of brief quotations
embodied in critical articles and reviews.

First Edition
First Printing, 2014

Book design by Donna Burch-Brown
Cover art: iStockphoto.com/12630236/ingmar wesemann
Cover design by Ellen Lawson
Editing by Connie Hill

Llewellyn Publications is a registered trademark of Llewellyn Worldwide Ltd.

Library of Congress Cataloging-in-Publication Data

Wojton, Djuna.
  Karmic choices : how making the right decisions can create enduring joy /
Djuna Wojton. — First edition
     pages cm
  Includes bibliographical references and index.
  ISBN 978-0-7387-3616-7
1. Karma. 2. Change (Psychology)—Miscellanea. 3. Mental healing. 4. Mind
and body—Miscellanea. 5. Success—Psychological aspects—Miscellanea. I.
Title.
  BF1045.K37.W64   2014
  158.1—dc23   2013036334

Llewellyn Worldwide Ltd. does not participate in, endorse, or have any authority
or responsibility concerning private business transactions between our authors
and the public.
  All mail addressed to the author is forwarded, but the publisher cannot, unless
specifically instructed by the author, give out an address or phone number.
  Any Internet references contained in this work are current at publication time,
but the publisher cannot guarantee that a specific location will continue to be
maintained. Please refer to the publisher's website for links to authors' websites
and other sources.

Llewellyn Publications
A Division of Llewellyn Worldwide Ltd.
2143 Wooddale Drive
Woodbury, MN 55125-2989
www.llewellyn.com

Printed in the United States of America

Dedication

To Debbie, Helen, Joseph, Maria, and Tasha.
Friendship is sacred.

Other Books by Djuna Wojton

*Karmic Healing: Clearing Past-Life Blocks to
Present-Day Love, Health, and Happiness*
Crossing Press, 2006

Disclaimer

The exercises and meditations in this book are not a substitute for medical or psychiatric care. The processes are challenging, best accomplished by those who are emotionally well balanced. Please seek appropriate help if you have a problem. If you are currently in therapy, consult with your therapist before exploring karmic choices.

All of the names of the clients and details of their circumstances mentioned in the book have been changed to protect their privacy.

Please note that all parts of this book are copyrighted. You may only record the meditations for your personal use.

Contents

List of Exercises xvii

Introduction: Are You Ready to Shift? / 1

Karma 2

Karmic Choices 4

Karmic Patterns 5

Karmic Pattern Three-Step Formula 6

Taking Control of Your Time 9

My Story 10

You Can Do Things You Never Imagined 13

Your Karmic Workbook 14

Living a Life You Love 15

Chapter One: Choose Now / 17

Choosing Life 17

Reaping What You Sow 21

Your Automatic Responses (*Samskaras*) 22

Patience Is a Virtue 35

Chapter Two: Choose Relief / 37

The Cause of Suffering *(Kleishas)* 38

1. Ignorance in Your Life (*Avidya*) 39

2. Ego in Your Life (*Asmita*) 48

3. Unhealthy Attachment in Your Life (*Raga*) 51

4. Repulsion in Your Life (*Dvesha*) 56

5. Death in Your Life (*Abhinivesha*) 63

Unraveling Distorted Perceptions (*Kleishas*) 66

Chapter Three: Choose Growth / 69

Choosing Trust 70

The Karmic Pattern Formula 73

1. Clarify: Locating and Examining
   a Karmic Pattern 74

2. Clear: Identifying Your Spiritual Lessons 82

3. Create: Uncovering New Actions 90

The Karmic Pattern Formula in Action 95

Chapter Four: Choose Integrity / 97

The Importance of Integrity 97

Unspoken Contracts 102

Maintaining Integrity (*Yamas*) 110

Restored Wholeness 116

Chapter Five: Choose Purpose / 119

Your Heart's Desire 119

Michel's Story 120

Living Life with Purpose 123

Living Purposefully (*Niyamas*) 129

Being Purposeful 150

Chapter Six: Choose Clarity / 151

The Law of Attraction 151

Using the Karmic Intentions Formula 155

1. Desires: True and False 156

2. Clarifying What You Want 157

3. Setting an Intention by Treasure Mapping 160

4. Setting a Time Frame   163

5. Taking Action   165

6. Determination   166

7. The Price You Pay   167

Karmic Intentions Formula Recap   179

Chapter Seven: Choose Action / 181

Your Resistance   181

Perfect Scenario   188

The Forces of Change   201

Being in Action   208

Chapter Eight: Choose Love / 209

The Reality about Love   209

Relationships Begin with You   212

Love Straight Talk   226

Love Is Tested   232

Love Is Always Present   246

Afterword: Choose Completion / 247

Suggested Reading   251

Glossary   255

Index   259

Acknowledgments   265

Exercises

Chapter One

Exercise: Knowing Your Automatic Responses 25

Exercise: Reaching the Root Cause of Your Fear 27

Exercise: Upgrading Your Program 30

Exercise: Learning to Self-Soothe 33

Exercise: Breathing Meditation 34

Exercise: Other Ways to Self-Soothe 34

Chapter Two

Exercise: Transforming Asmita 50

Exercise: When Do You Become Attached? 53

Exercise: Getting Back on the Horse 58

Exercise: Knowing Your Range 63

Exercise: Releasing Abhinivesha 65

Chapter Three

Exercise: Step One: Clarify—Identifying Unwanted
Conditions 81

Exercise: Step Two: Clear—Identifying Your Spiritual
Lessons 88

Exercise: Step Three: Create—Identifying Your New
Actions 94

Chapter Four

Exercise: Integrity Checklist 100

Exercise: Restoring Your Integrity 101

Exercise: Rebalancing Unspoken Contracts
   with Others   104
Exercise: Rebalancing Your Contract with Earth   109
Journaling Exercise: Yamas in Your Life   112

Chapter Five

Exercise: Checking In with Your Purpose   124
Journaling Exercise: Niyamas in Your Life   131
Exercise: Find Your Purpose   141

Chapter Six

Exercise: Having, Being, Doing   159
Exercise: Karmic Timing   164
Exercise: Karmic Price Tags   170
Exercise: Self-Worth Tips   172
Exercise: Arrogance   172
Exercise: Buying It   173

Chapter Seven

Exercise: Gaining Insight   183
Exercise: How to Use the Yamas to Change   196
Exercise: Turning Points—Discover Your Style   205

Chapter Eight

Exercise: Checking In with You   218
Exercise: Loving Yourself Checklist   219
Exercise: Love Being In Communication   230
Exercise: Love Is a Great Teacher   240

Introduction

ARE YOU READY TO SHIFT?

You want some kind of change in your life, but you can't seem to make it happen. Maybe you placed your dreams on the back burner so many years ago that you've forgotten what they are. You never ran that marathon, wrote a novel, took a world cruise, or learned to sail.

Or could it be that, after years of marriage, you are unaware that you've drifted apart from your spouse? Or, perhaps, being single for so long, you have resigned yourself to never having a partner?

Or maybe it's time for a career change. You're bored, working at a dead-end job just trying to make ends meet, but haven't pursued anything truly satisfying.

It's always easier to find reasons and excuses for why you can't do what you want.

If you're willing to open up to more satisfaction in some area of life, be it in your career, relationships, or self-expression, *Karmic Choices* will show you how. You'll discover how to get unstuck by healing old issues, connecting with your soul awareness, and designing a plan for a fulfilling future. Its case studies and stories illustrate spiritual teachings and principles that will empower you to get back on track. Questionnaires will prepare you to work on your core issues. Finally, exercises, meditations, and the three-step Karmic Pattern Formula will help you release the blockages and limiting beliefs that keep you immobilized so that you can take the steps you need to create a life you love.

Like an explorer venturing into unknown territory and making new discoveries, you'll see the world with wiser eyes, and each chapter will support and nurture your growing self-awareness and confidence. Your experience of who you are will expand as your options increase, and as a result, you'll be able to accomplish more and thereby be more satisfied with your life than you ever imagined possible.

Karma

Karma is a Sanskrit word that means "action." Clearly, then, you can't avoid karma, since life is composed of action.

You've probably heard the saying, "What you sow, you will reap." Basically, this spiritual law means that you are responsible for your actions and their consequences. This is the same spiritual law defined by the term *karma*. With karma, your positive actions have constructive results and your negative actions have destructive results. As such, karma can be viewed as the combined set of circumstances that either allows you to move forward in life or holds you back.

You may wonder why bad things happen to good people and how karma applies to them. Here's where the theory of reincarnation comes into play. Since ancient times, many cultures have believed that birth and death are part of a continuous cycle through which a soul can heal and transform. Buddhism, Hinduism, and many earth-based religions include reincarnation in their doctrines. Past-life expert and best-selling author Dr. Brian Weiss claims that "even Christianity embraced reincarnation until Emperor Constantine deleted references of past lives from the Bible in the fourth century."[1]

Reincarnation espouses the belief that your soul chooses to be born on earth to learn and experience, because life offers new opportunities to grow. Sometimes such opportunity—as the result of karma—comes in the form of challenging circumstances to help you learn the impact of your past actions on others and thereby "balance the scales." In the process, these difficult situations also force you to develop strength or upgrade your character. As such, I call the wisdom gleaned from these opportunities *spiritual lessons,* as ultimately you are here to discover your true divine nature.

---

1. Brian Weiss, MD, *Many Lives, Many Masters* (Simon & Schuster, 1988), 35.

At this moment, your life is a culmination of all the karma created by the consequences of past actions and choices. Thus, the exercises, stories, and meditations in this book will help you to make choices in keeping with the spiritual law that "as you sow, so shall you reap." *Karmic Choices* will help you to become aware that you are not alone, but interconnected to everyone and everything, for it is with such awareness that you will create positive karma for yourself and for the world.

Karmic Choices

How you live your life matters. If you have made conscious choices and generated positive actions in some areas of life, and those choices and actions are life affirming for you and others, you will harvest the rewards by experiencing success and fulfillment in those areas. I call these choices and actions "karmic choices."

By showing you how to work with the laws of karma, *Karmic Choices* will teach you how to achieve your goals so that everyone comes out a winner. People who focus only on their own goals and ignore the effects of their actions on others cause suffering for everyone and everything—not just for people, but for all life on the planet. So you'll discover how to view your aspirations within a broader perspective; you'll expand your scope and see the bigger picture, for when you consider how your decisions affect your community, the environment, and the world, you make better choices.

You'll learn ethical precepts I've included from various translations of *The Yoga Sutras of Patanjali*, an ancient sacred text of Indian philosophy. These precepts that have been used in India for two millennia will help you be at peace with yourself, your family, and your community. Rather than just providing a list of dos and don'ts, this code will help you cultivate your spirituality by developing qualities of honesty, integrity, and nonviolence. These principles will enable you to delve into the inner workings of your mind, uncover limiting belief systems, and change your automatic ways of responding to life. You'll be able to replace agitation with calm so that you can transform the way you relate to the world. I've provided a glossary at the end of the book to help you learn the definitions of foreign or unfamiliar terms.

Karmic Patterns

Have you ever caught yourself experiencing a similar distressing situation over and over again? The cast of characters and scenes has changed, but the theme is the same? The experience is like that of watching a television rerun: it's boring and you know the outcome, but you keep watching it anyway. Such persistent distressful situations are caused by automatic behaviors that I call *karmic patterns*.

As mentioned, your time on earth offers new challenges and unique experiences, all in the context of learning about yourself. In turn, the more self-aware you are, the better your ability to respond consciously, rather than reactively, to such experiences. You *can* train yourself to release unwanted and self-destructive tendencies. Even if you feel something is beyond your control, you *can* choose how to respond.

Say, for instance, that you keep finding yourself in relationships in which you're the giver and the other is the taker, and you end up feeling angry and resentful as a result. Unfortunately, you will continue to attract such "takers" until you consciously accept this aspect of your behavior. Perhaps your lesson is to create healthy boundaries—not to sacrifice your needs for others, but to say no when appropriate—and learn how to receive.

When you consciously make choices that are different from those you've made in your past, even if you attract the same set of circumstances, you'll have learned your lesson, be free to respond in healthier ways, and ultimately experience a more positive outcome.

Karmic Pattern Three-Step Formula

Over the years I've developed and taught a three-step formula that has helped many people release karmic patterns, heal past wounds, and create new beginnings. Now I want to share this process with you.

1. **Clarify.** Becoming aware that a situation is repetitive, and recalling its roots, is the first step to releasing it.

2. **Clear.** Understanding the spiritual lesson attached to the karmic pattern you identified in the previous step frees you to rewrite the script for the life you want.

3. **Create**. Committing to take a specific action that works for the highest good of all helps you upgrade your behavior and unleash your passion.

Here's an example of how the process works. Nadine came to my office for a reading because she was upset with her boss, John. They were in the business of selling art to hotels and other corporate clients. Nadine loved talking with people, so she thought she'd be successful at her new job, which entailed cold-calling clients, following up, and then wining and dining potential buyers.

Nadine had always thought she was a good communicator, but a recent confrontation with John in her office had made her realize that the topic of money was one she avoided.

Nadine and John had been friends for ten years when he invited her to be a full partner in his art consulting business. She accepted, and they both agreed that while Nadine was learning the business, he would take a percentage of the commissions she earned on the paintings and prints she sold. Since they were old friends, Nadine assumed the percentage rate would be fair. They never discussed the details, and she never signed a contract.

When she got her first check and saw the huge chunk John had taken she was livid. "For the past two months, I've busted my behind working sixty-hour weeks while John was hardly around," she said as her face flushed. "I came into the office every weekend while he left town to stay at his beach house. I broke the record and tripled sales, and yet he took most of the money. It isn't fair."

When she told me her story, it was clear to me that a karmic pattern was surfacing; overreaction is a clue that a karmic pattern is buried and you are ready to release it. So applying

Karmic Choice's first step, **clarify**, I coached her to close her eyes and breathe deeply.

"When did a similar situation occur in your life?" I asked.

Tears streamed down her face. "This is just like what happened in my marriage. My ex-husband and I shared a joint bank account. We were both working, yet he spent most of our money. He not only paid child support to his three children from his previous marriage but also sent extra money every month. He went way overboard, affecting our own financial security. I thought if I said anything, I'd sound selfish. So I stuffed how I felt, and eventually our marriage fell apart."

As Nadine began to identify and release her karmic pattern, the second step, **clear**, came into play. I asked Nadine to go within herself and ask, "What is the spiritual lesson attached to this pattern?"

Nadine took a deep breath and replied, "I also realize that I've had this hidden fear about standing up for myself in a relationship. I thought I was communicating, but I was really avoiding bringing up subjects that felt uncomfortable. I jumped into this business partnership without even a contract because I was working with a friend and I assumed he wouldn't take advantage of me."

Nadine then shared how she felt she needed to change. "I need to take responsibility for what I want and not take for granted that others will take care of me. Just because someone is my friend, doesn't mean he or she knows what I need. Instead of suppressing what I want to say, I need to be honest, open, and straightforward when I communicate. I affirm that I can speak my truth to people."

Next came **create**, the third step. I asked, "What action do you need to take that would be good for you and everyone involved?"

Nadine knew what she needed to do, not just to benefit her, but to help John as well. She needed to call and confront John about their financial arrangement.

When I asked Nadine to commit to a date, she answered, "By the end of the week."

A week later, Nadine phoned me to tell me the outcome of her conversation with John. "It went beautifully. John broke down the expenses, so I was able to see the split in the check very clearly. We agreed we needed to write a contract so my responsibilities, time commitments, and compensations are clearly spelled out."

Nadine hadn't been able to express herself freely in her marriage. Years later, she became enmeshed in another situation in which she could learn to respond to a partner in a healthier way. When you "get" the spiritual lesson being offered to you, you become free to make better choices.

Taking Control of Your Time

If you are out of touch with your priorities, it's natural to fall into the trap of simply reacting to the situations of the day. You notice the dust balls gathering on the floor and get the vacuum out of the closet. The phone rings. When you answer, your mother says, "Honey, can you help me with this computer glitch?" Immediately you've been recruited as tech help. The dog won't stop barking, so you hang up the phone to get the leash. While walking the dog, you work up an appetite. You look in the refrigerator. Seeing nothing is there, you drive to the grocery store. And so it goes.

Of course there will always be circumstances that are unplanned, that may require immediate attention. But, if you aren't focused on what is most important to you, it's easy to get in the habit of reacting to the day's events so that, by late evening, you wonder where the time went. You were going to accomplish something like rewriting your résumé. Or you were going to do something for yourself like practicing yoga, meditating, or jogging in the park. Instead, the demands of the outer world took precedence over your inner convictions.

Karmic Choices helps you learn how to overcome this trap and to spend your energy productively. You'll examine every area of your life, uncovering what's not working. Whether it's an emotionally draining relationship, unproductive conversations, or out-of-control spending habits, you will discover habits in your life that you need to change. *Karmic Choices* gives you the tools to stop wasting time and take control by designing an exciting, interesting, and productive life.

My Story

I know what it's like to yearn for a full, meaningful life. I spent years feeling helpless and afraid because I was out of touch with what I wanted and needed. I felt disconnected from my body and was unaware of my emotions. My thoughts raced,

I felt anxious most of the time, and I couldn't concentrate. I developed this way of being in my childhood.

My mother was overprotective. During the snowy winters in Cleveland, Ohio, sidewalks would be covered with ice and snow. As I bundled up for my walk to school, Mom would tower over me, saying, "Be careful, or you'll slip and break a leg and be crippled for life." Hearing those words repeated over the years, I began to doubt that my feet would ever carry me over the ice.

I was forbidden to skate, ride a bike, or climb the monkey bars. Mom was convinced I would have an accident or poke my eyes out and become blind. I was twelve and still riding an oversized tricycle. If I wasn't sitting at the kitchen table, I was in danger. While I was playing with my Barbie doll on the driveway one day, my mother yelled out to me, "You'll develop shingles." Swimming in the community pool could cause tuberculosis or leukemia. Touching the stove might create third-degree burns, and I wouldn't dare light the oven for fear I'd blow up the house.

Listening to my mother's fearful predictions year after year took its toll. I felt helpless and lacked confidence most of the time, nearly failing home economics in junior high school. It was as if I had become endowed with some horrible telekinetic power: all I had to do was sit down at a sewing machine, and instantly the needle would break. The bobbin would become so entangled with thread that it would be unusable. As I approached the stove in cooking class, cakes rising in the oven would fall, sautés burn, and sauces bubble over.

My dad was supportive of me, but he wasn't available most of the time. He was a hard-working, hard-drinking man. He welded Buicks together on an assembly line by day and avoided my mother at night by drinking himself to sleep.

Meanwhile, as I was struggling with my fears and ineptitude, the world was rapidly changing, making it easier for me to seek help. In the late 1960s, the philosophies of the East were being brought to the West. Many people were seeking alternatives to the traditional and materialistic values of our society, and I was one of them.

I wanted to find my inner light switch, turn it on, and shine brightly. I began practicing yoga and stopped eating junk food. After a few months, my weak, clumsy body transformed into one of strength and coordination. Then learning to consciously detach from my racing, judgmental thoughts brought me peace. My spiritual quests began with yoga and whetted my appetite for more. I went on to study a variety of spiritual traditions and to gather much wisdom. Following my spiritual path led me to study yoga in India and shamanic healing in the Amazon jungle. I've been able to interview famous New Age authors for my radio show, belly dance in Egypt, and read tarot cards while cruising through the Mediterranean—things I thought I'd never do! Such activities may sound commonplace now, but back in the twentieth century, they were unusual and adventurous.

But most important, my studies in yoga, metaphysics, and holistic therapies have enabled me to make a difference in people's lives. The processes I developed in this book first helped me. They freed me of my mother's fear so that I could do things she told me I'd never do—like take long rides on my two-wheeler mountain bike, go cross-country skiing, or even stand on my head. Now I want to share the wisdom I have gleaned with you.

You Can Do Things You Never Imagined

I've now helped thousands of people create positive life changes by rediscovering what they want and becoming empowered to create it. They have been able to learn what one of my teachers always said: "You either have the result you want or the reasons why you don't."

Maybe an overprotective mother didn't raise you. You may or may not find inaction to be a problem. But there is probably some area in your life where you feel limited in your expression. It could be that you want deeper intimacy with your mate or family members. Perhaps you fear asking for help but are tired of doing everything alone. Maybe you can't speak in front of large groups but need to if you expect to be promoted.

Applying the wisdom I've gathered from my studies, *Karmic Choices* will help you pinpoint the areas where your fear stops you. You'll learn how to recognize and acknowledge your fear and not be limited by it. You'll then discover how to act courageously despite your fears and to choose behaviors that will lead you to a life that you ultimately love.

Your Karmic Workbook

To obtain the full benefit from this book, you'll need a journal or large sketchbook in which to record your responses to the exercises and to document your progress as you grow and change. Make sure you choose a notebook that is at least 8½" by 11" with unlined, blank pages that can hold a variety of media. Or you may want to use your laptop, if it has a drawing program and if you're comfortable using the technology.

Please also keep these items on hand as you read this book, and use them to help you unleash your creativity:

- Old magazines, along with scissors, glue, and Scotch tape to make collages and treasure maps.

- Colored markers, pencils, or pens to make writing exercises more pleasurable and fun.

- A digital recorder to record and play back meditations.

- Either an appointment calendar or PDA to help you plan and manage your projects.

- Soothing music to accompany the meditations and support you in relaxing.

- A deck of Rider-Waite tarot cards to enhance your ability to visualize and develop your intuition. During some meditations, you'll learn to interact with tarot archetypes so that they become your guides to the inner realms.

But you will benefit even if you don't follow the exercises, for you can learn from the entertaining stories and examples.

Living a Life You Love

As a counselor, I hear many people complain that their jobs are making them stressed and killing their spirits, yet they stay. Some cling to loveless marriages. Others continue to indulge in addictions that harm their health. It is difficult to break old patterns and habits—it's so much easier to stay in your comfort zone. If you are willing to do the work and look within, however, you will be rewarded. Boredom, resignation, stress, and fear will transform into passion as your life becomes a grand adventure.

Spiritual growth and change are as magical as caterpillars turning into butterflies. You'll go through a rebirth experience as old ways of thinking, being, and doing fall away and a new sense of self emerges. Then, feeling more joyful and productive than ever, you will step into your power.

Chapter One

CHOOSE NOW

The magic of life exists in the present moment, yet people have a natural tendency to avoid being there by unconsciously clinging to past hurts and failures. Because the body, mind, and spirit are holistically interconnected, these unresolved issues could manifest as anxiety, self-destructive reactions, or even physical pain. When we heal and release these outworn negative experiences, we can be fully aware in the now and thereby make better choices. In the process of letting go of resentments, fears, and old ways of being, new openings for peace, productivity, and vitality become available.

Choosing Life

When Ciara was diagnosed with type 2 diabetes, she felt as though she'd been given a death sentence, since her sister had suffered a painful demise from this disease. In her early thirties, Ciara's life was spinning out of control. She was desperate to do something to get herself back on track, so she scheduled an appointment for a soul-healing session.

When Ciara arrived at my office, I saw that she was five feet four inches tall and weighed three hundred pounds. Her weight was a tremendous burden, for it was painful even to walk. She was also on medication for asthma, diabetes, and anxiety, which all seemed to zap her vitality. She said she was exhausted most of the time and didn't have energy to do much of anything. She wondered if she even had the strength to go on living.

Ciara's weight had been a lifelong issue. She had never known food to be a source of sustenance, and she'd had eating disorders since childhood. While growing up, Ciara had always seen her mother obsessed with losing weight, and even as a young girl, Ciara would go on fad diets with her mother and be her weight-loss buddy. What Ciara was given to eat depended on her mother's moods, so regular meals were nonexistent.

Some days, Ciara would be deprived a normal breakfast, lunch, and dinner; her sole midday meal would be a half a grapefruit and a few saltine crackers. But a few days later, when her mother felt they needed a treat, they'd drive to Howard Johnson's and indulge in hot fudge sundaes.

Not only did they alternate starving and binging for years, but Ciara's mother used her blood pressure medication as a diuretic to lose weight, and forced ten-year-old Ciara to take it as well.

In her healing session, Ciara drifted into a state of deep relaxation. I asked her if she felt any pain in her body connected to her mother.

Tears streamed down her cheeks as she replied, "I feel like there is barbed wire wrapped around my stomach."

I placed my hands on Ciara's stomach to give her Reiki spiritual healing and asked her if she could forgive her mother. In her now-relaxed state, Ciara took a broader perspective. She said that she understood that her mother had been emotionally ill and therefore didn't know how to take care of her.

Ciara took a deep breath and sighed. "Yes, I can forgive her."

I asked Ciara to work with me and visualize clearing the blockage. Ciara imagined the barbed wire turning into leaves that were then blown away by a gentle wind as I continued to channel healing energy to her. She reported a sense of peace filling every cell of her being and feeling lighter and relieved. I affirmed that she had much to live for and that she had much support from the Higher Power.

I then asked Ciara if she had learned something from this experience.

"I need to stop blaming my mother for my condition and take responsibility for my health," she said with determination. "I'm not a victim."

In that moment, I knew that Ciara's life would take a new course.

At the end of her session, I reinforced that Ciara needed to seek out a nutritionist, a psychologist, and medical support to help her lose weight safely.

As she left my office with an apparent sense of purpose, she declared, "I want to live!"

However, weeks went by, and nothing changed until one fateful day.

Ciara struck up a conversation with a woman on the subway, something she didn't normally do. The stranger told Ciara that many people had breakthrough weight-loss results after having gastric bypass surgery and gave her the office number of a well-respected specialist in the area who could perform the operation. Ciara thanked the stranger for the information. She had never considered surgery an option.

At home, Ciara researched gastric bypass surgery on the Internet and found statistics stating that many of those who'd undergone the surgery were cured of type 2 diabetes. At that moment, Ciara knew this was what she wanted to do.

The next day, Ciara called the specialist for an appointment. Thereafter, she became committed to having the procedure. In fact, she had never felt so fervently dedicated to doing anything as she did to having this operation. Her passion gave her the strength to persist through all the preliminary tests; she needed to receive approval from a psychologist, be checked by a cardiologist, and have an ultrasound. The biggest hurdle was getting the insurance clearance. Much seemed out of her control, yet Ciara became unstoppable.

The next time I heard from Ciara was two years later. I hardly recognized her when I saw the beautiful woman standing on my doorstep.

"You look fabulous," I said, my jaw literally dropping.

"I lost a hundred and thirty pounds!" she said.

Ciara told me about the operation and went on to say that she had changed her eating habits. "Food is now nourishment!" she said. "I'll never diet again. I now eat healthy meals. I've even reversed the diabetes. I have so much more energy; I can do things again."

She proudly extended her left hand, showing off her engagement ring. "I have a new life!"

Reaping What You Sow

Ciara's story is a dramatic example of how her past affected her as an adult. It took a crisis for her to stop living at the mercy of her mother's eating habits and to change her life, but when she made the deliberate, intentional attempt to take control of her health, she was able to steer a different course for her future, avoiding further disaster and creating a better way of living. You don't have to hit rock bottom, however, before you can transform.

As difficult as it may be to accept, everything that happens to you results from choices you made in the past. It's often easy to acknowledge your own role in the areas of life that are working well, but hard to accept in the areas that aren't. It's tough to admit that you chose to go into debt, get divorced, or be stuck in a dead-end job. But once you take total responsibility for all the choices you've made—good and bad, conscious and automatic—you regain your power and inner peace.

But I need to define "you." You are neither your body nor your personality. You are not your thoughts; you are not your emotions. The real you is the soul, which is eternal and divine and is connected to everyone and everything in the universe. Your authentic self exists in the silence between thoughts and in the emptiness between each inhale and exhale.

We are all one, but there is something that separates us into individuals and makes us each unique. Your ego, or personality, gives you individuality. Your soul is unlimited, while your ego has limitations. The soul lives in the present, but the ego is preoccupied with the past or future.

Your soul has incarnated in a body and personality. Your conscious mind is a function of your personality, and you express your ego though it. You are here on earth on an evolutionary journey to gain wisdom and discover your divine nature. Sometimes the personality and unconscious mind are aligned with your soul's purpose, but at other times they are off track.

Your Automatic Responses (Samskaras)

You make choices every minute of the day whether you realize it or not, including what to think about, what to feel, and how to react to situations you encounter. Each moment offers a variety of ways to respond to life's circumstances. If you are stuck in a traffic jam, you could relax and watch the clouds sail across the sky or you could throw a temper tantrum. While waiting in a long checkout line in the grocery store, you could get annoyed or strike up a friendly conversation with the person behind you. For better or worse, your past shapes your present and future.

Adding to that, we are creatures of habit, repeating behaviors until they become automatic. *Samskaras* are what the yogis call these unconscious thought processes, which include making judgments, evaluations, and assumptions and automatic emotional reactions. We are at the mercy of our automatic responses unless we make a conscious effort to be in the now. Reacting mechanically to life limits our creativity and restricts our ability to be fully self-expressed and productive. Fortunately, we have the power to change our automatic, negative responses into positive, constructive actions, but this takes practice.

If you are willing to make the effort, you can begin transforming your life. Simply make the commitment to be aware, and you will be able to replace habitual behaviors with mindfulness. You will be more in touch with your soul, and life will take on a feeling of greater purpose and ease.

To start, use the following stories, questionnaires, and exercises to help you discover how past experiences may be influencing your present.

What Needs to Change?

Together, your personality traits and habits influence your automatic responses. A habit is a simple act that you do over and over, such as always eating breakfast by seven or falling asleep at eleven. In turn, your habits crystallize into such a routine that your stomach growls if you don't eat at the usual hour and you feel drowsy if you stay up past your bedtime.

In every area of your life, you have good and bad habits. Good health habits may include upholding a daily exercise regime, a nutritious diet, or regular meditation. Bad work habits may include forgetting appointments, ignoring phone calls, or keeping a messy desk. A positive social habit may be sending a thank-you note to someone who gives you a gift, while a negative one may be interrupting people while they speak.

Personality traits are repeated behaviors that become part of your identity. Always being late is an example. I once had a fitness instructor who was never on time. The class was scheduled to start at nine every Tuesday morning, but she'd make her grand entrance each week at ten after nine. During the first couple of classes, she'd apologize for keeping everyone waiting, blaming her late arrival on traffic problems. But after a month, she stopped apologizing. This was her unspoken way of saying that class would always start at ten after nine, despite how it was listed on the schedule.

By the time she'd taken off her coat, set up her bench, gotten out her weights, and connected her iPod to the speakers, it was twenty after nine. This left us with only forty minutes of workout time, which to some was a blessing. To others, however, it was unacceptable. To make up for her tardiness, she'd teach class until twenty after ten, but most of the class had to leave at the top of the hour.

Class members who arrived early began to set up the instructor's bench to save time, while other members began to straggle in late, and some just got fed up and dropped out. When a new member joined our group and asked us about the class, someone would be sure to say, "It's a great class, but the instructor is always late." After time, the instructor created her own reputation and suffered the consequences of her actions: she was fired.

It is natural to become so dependent on habits and traits that you accept yesterday's actions as today's norm. But you are the one who chooses to act in certain ways, whether unconsciously or with awareness, and those choices influence how others perceive you.

Exercise:
Knowing Your Automatic Responses

The good news is that your habits and traits are the results of your choices, and they can be changed if you are willing to make the effort. You learned them and, therefore, can unlearn them—and learn new, better ones.

To do this, however, you first need to know what behaviors you'd like to change. Think about what behaviors negatively affect the quality of your life. Are you willing to take responsibility for those behaviors and change them?

Read through the lists of behaviors below and consider whether you have any of them. Then identify those behaviors that don't support your goals and objectives.

In the area of relationships:

- Do you automatically say yes to others' requests before thinking about whether you are committed to following through with those requests—making you a people pleaser?

- Are you a perfectionist to the point that no one is ever good enough for you?

- Does your need to be in control turn you into a power tripper?

- Are you a conflict avoider, ignoring issues that need to be addressed?

In the area of work:

- Are you disorganized?

- Do you waste too much energy talking about what you want to do instead of taking action?

- Are you a procrastinator?

- Do you bad-mouth your boss or coworkers?

In the area of health and well-being:

- Does impatience cause you to act recklessly?

- Do you overextend yourself and thereby feel burned out and drained?

- Are you an overeater?

- Do you have a problem asking for what you want?

Oftentimes, a negative trait serves you because it masks a hidden fear. If you procrastinate, thereby letting opportunities pass you by, for example, that may signify that you are afraid of either success or failure, and such an action would prevent you from experiencing either one.

There may be a reason why you are messy. If you were organized, you'd stop spinning your wheels. You'd have more time and energy to devote to a creative project. But then your creativity would be open to public scrutiny, and maybe you fear being criticized.

Or perhaps you use overeating to stuff your anger and resentment. If you use food to numb your feelings, you don't have to feel the pain. If you had to deal with the pain, you'd regain your power over the situation that caused it, and maybe that scares you.

Exercise:
Reaching the Root Cause of Your Fear

The following is a two-step exercise. Step one is a meditation that will enable you to discover the fear hidden beneath each of the negative personality traits you have identified in your life. Step two is a journaling exercise that will help you better understand that fear and rise above it.

Step One: Meditation

It's best to make an audio recording of this meditation. Take a couple of minutes to pause after each question to allow enough time for the information to "come through" to you. Don't rush. The whole process should take about fifteen minutes. Perform the meditation for each negative trait you identified, with the intention of going to the source of the trait. You can practice this meditation as many times as you need to explore as many traits as you like.

Begin recording the following script:

Relax into a comfortable position. Close your eyes and take a deep breath. Feel your breath move through your body like a gentle wave. When you inhale, inhale peace. Now exhale, and let go of any tension. Continue breathing deeply this way for a minute or two as you release all your concerns of the day. Allow your thoughts to float away like feathery clouds in a blue sky.

Begin to feel a sense of lightness, a sense of peace and oneness. Enjoy this precious moment of relaxation.

Now allow yourself to go deeper. As you count from three down to one, let this feeling of relaxation double.

Three. Go deeper and deeper.

Two. Become more and more relaxed.

One. Your relaxation has totally doubled now.

Now, imagine you are at home, sitting in your favorite chair. In front of you is a giant television screen. In your hand is a remote control. When you press the button on the remote, the *source* of your negative personality trait appears on the screen. Trust what comes on the screen and view the information in a way that's easy and comfortable.

What do you see? Is it a word or sentence? Is it an image? Is it a scene? What fear is your negative trait hiding?

Turn up the volume. Can you hear a message?

Now open yourself deeper into your intuition and consider the following:

- How would your life change if you didn't have this fear?
- Would you welcome those changes?
- What person or persons wouldn't like you to change?

Give thanks for the insights you have received.

After a few more moments, count from one up to five. On the count of five, you'll be wide awake, totally refreshed, and feeling good.

One … two … three … four … five. Open your eyes, wide. You are wide awake.

End your recording.

Step Two: Journaling

Take as much time as you need to write down in your journal any impressions, feelings, or words of guidance you received. Now that you know what you're afraid of, you can begin to play with it. Exaggerating your fear, in particular, can show you how ridiculous it is. Use the following exercise to do just that and diffuse the power of your fear.

Write the answer to the following questions on a clean sheet of paper in your journal:

- If your fear didn't stop you, what is the worst that could happen? Imagine the worst-case scenario as if it were a scene in a soap opera. Who are the main characters?

Pretend you are writing a script for television and have fun writing this scene out as a melodrama.

- Look objectively at what you wrote in the previous step. How could you reduce the likelihood of this worst-case scenario from occurring? What traits would you need? Would you be able to cope? Whom could you count on for help? Would you have enough support?

Now examine your potential losses realistically to decide if this fear is worth holding onto. Once you've cleared away the fear, it will be easier to change your negative trait.

Exercise: Upgrading Your Program

Now pick one of the negative traits you recognized in yourself that you would like to transform, and make it the title on a blank page of your journal. For example, write "Setting Boundaries and Saying No." Then take the following steps to change this negative trait into something positive and automatic:

- Create a positive statement that affirms your ability to overcome this quality. It could be something like "I can say no to others without losing love" or "I say yes only to what I'm committed to doing."

- Write down your affirmation in your journal ten times a day for twenty-one days, or until it becomes your new automatic response.

- Before getting out of bed each morning and then before going to sleep at night, say your affirmation out loud to yourself, take a deep breath, pause, and repeat this process ten times.

- Write down your positive statement on note cards and place them in different areas of your house where you can see and be reminded of the affirmation.

This exercise may seem excessive, but the actual writing and speaking of your affirmation frequently and over a long period of time will help you reprogram your subconscious mind.

Quick Fixes

Many times our negative personality traits have a component of anxiety attached to them. When we are stressed or upset, we tend to search for a quick fix to make us feel better. Instead of dealing with the unpleasant emotions in the moment, it's common for us to suppress or deny them by drinking too much caffeine or alcohol, smoking, overeating, or taking part in any number of other undesirable behaviors. We convince ourselves we want something because it was pleasant before, even though we do not actually need it in the present moment.

Here's an example of how an urge to eat comfort food was a quick fix in an upsetting situation. Jenna came into my office for a healing. She was suffering from lower back pain and had trouble sleeping at night.

When I asked Jenna what was wrong, she began to cry and said, "Yesterday I ate a large three-cheese pepperoni pizza for dinner. My limit is usually two slices, but I wolfed down the whole thing. To top it off, I had sticky-toffee pudding sundae topped with whipped cream and half a cup of crème de menthe for dessert. I thought eating my favorite foods would make me feel better. It did in the moment, but I wound up feeling sick the whole night."

I coached Jenna to close her eyes and take a deep breath. Then I asked, "With whom are you upset?"

Jenna resumed crying as she told me that she was having difficulty dealing with her stepbrother, George. Her father had died over a year ago and Jenna resented the fact that George had been appointed executor of the will and was bequeathed a larger part of the estate than she. He wasn't even related to her father by blood, so it seemed unfair that he would receive any inheritance. Jenna took another deep breath.

"What are you feeling?" I asked.

"I'm so mad at my father, but haven't allowed myself to feel it. How could I be angry with him? He's dead. Besides, I was always taught that nice girls don't get angry. I couldn't talk to my friends about the will because I didn't want to seem petty. So I just keep stuffing my feelings, pretending they'll go away."

Jenna also said she felt bitter about the fact that George was so unorganized that he was taking too long to settle the estate. It was nearing the end of the year, and for tax purposes, Jenna needed a detailed accounting of the modest amount she would receive. But anytime she e-mailed George requesting a complete financial statement, he would reply that he'd send the report next week. But as next week turned into the next month, the report never came.

George wouldn't answer her phone calls and stopped replying to her e-mails. Since he lived across the country, it was impossible for her just to drop in on him. Jenna's anger had been festering for months, yet she wasn't even aware that she was enraged. She felt powerless.

During her session, Jenna gave herself permission to release her rage at her stepbrother and father. She had fun sticking out her tongue and roaring like a lion. She crayoned two sheets of blank paper using bold strokes of orange and red.

Afterward, she reported feeling peaceful and lighter. I applied Reiki to her lower back, and her pain went away as well. With her power restored, she came to the conclusion that it would be better if a lawyer handled the situation with George. She left the office choosing to feel empowered and content.

Exercise:
Learning to Self-Soothe

Take a moment to think about those situations in which you go on automatic pilot and lose self-control. For example, in what situations do you rely on external things to temporarily comfort you? To help you get in touch with such situations in your daily life, consider this list of compulsive behaviors and ask yourself what circumstances might cause you to react in the following ways:

- buying things you don't need
- raiding the refrigerator, even though you're not hungry
- drinking too many alcoholic beverages
- spending a night watching mindless television
- smoking cigarettes
- binging on sugar
- using recreational drugs to escape

Once you've isolated some of the situations that trigger you to make negative choices, you can substitute the following self-soothing techniques to empower yourself when you feel stressed. You can use these techniques at work, at home, in the gym, or anywhere you can claim a private space for a couple of minutes.

Exercise:
Breathing Meditation

Close your eyes. Take a moment to center yourself by slowly inhaling through your nose. Then exhale slowly through your mouth. Place all your awareness on your breath, as you repeat this process over and over. Become your breath. Easy inhalation. Easy exhalation. Do this consciously for twenty breaths to restore peace and calm.

Exercise:
Other Ways to Self-Soothe

Here are some other self-soothing activities for you to try. Feel free to add your ideas to the list.

- **Use your body.** Exercise to accelerate your heart rate by jogging or walking in nature, stretching, swimming, or practicing yoga.
- **Be playful.** Engage in team sports, give your pet extra attention, or solve puzzles.
- **Nurture your environment.** Clean your car inside and out; put your house in order; remove clutter from drawers, desktops, and closets; organize your garage; do gardening or landscaping.
- **Be creative.** Sing or play an instrument, paint or draw, dance, knit, or write in a journal.
- **Ease your mind.** Gaze at a fireplace or aquarium, pray, meditate, or chant.

Which activities will you add to your life? The key to changing an automatic response is pausing, thinking, and then practicing positive self-soothing activities instead of harmful ones until it becomes a habit. As mentioned, the process takes at least twenty-one days. Training yourself to respond positively is the same as learning any other discipline: it takes persistence and commitment.

Patience Is a Virtue

In this chapter, you discovered that your life is about choices. You became aware of the negative habits and personality traits that no longer serve you and have begun to transform them into positive attributes. You have put yourself on the road to being more aware, feeling more confident, and having wider access to conscious choices.

If you are new to doing spiritual work, however, be patient with yourself. Change happens over time. Just know that if you take committed action and do the work, you will be rewarded.

Chapter Two

CHOOSE RELIEF

The Yoga Sutras teach that *kleishas* are states of mind that distort your view of reality. Recognizing and addressing these misperceptions can help relieve suffering. Once you unravel the kleishas operating in your life, the benefits are enormous. You become in touch with your purpose and are then able to share your gifts and make positive contributions. Drama ceases to drain you emotionally, so you have more energy to use in creative ways. You feel more connected to others and part of a wider community. You're able to feel valued for what you do rather than the size of your income. Abundance becomes your natural state, for you know that spirit provides for all your needs.

The Cause of Suffering (*Kleishas*)

Suffering is inevitable because we don't live in an ideal world. Life is filled with ups and downs, and circumstances are constantly changing, so that many suffer anxiety, fear, or nervous tension on a daily basis.

During the course of your life, you are likely to experience physical pain and illness. You may also endure grief, disappointment, or depression. Even if you have a very happy life, you will suffer at the time of your death because it will be hard to leave it behind.

Studying with Sanskrit scholar and author Dr. Edwin Bryant helped me become clear on how the kleishas cause suffering and are impediments to spiritual growth. There are five major kleishas, which can distort our mind and perceptions, and affect how we think, feel, and act. The kleishas prevent us from achieving enlightenment and living up to our true potential. The five kleishas are as follows:

1. **Ignorance:** *Avidya.* The root kleisha is the first and main cause of all suffering. When we deny that our true nature is spiritual and divine, we live in ignorance. Believing the material reality is all that is real and thinking we are separate from people and the rest of the world perpetuates misery.

2. **Ego:** *Asmita.* When we identify with our personality or body, we become attached to a false identity. We pursue power, glamour, wealth, or fame because we think our status is who we really are. Or we feel powerless and succumb to depression and addictions or

waste our lives doing things that don't really matter to us because we're not in touch with our true self.

3. **Attachment: *Raga*.** When we experience pleasure, we desire to experience it again. When the experience is unavailable, we feel pain. Or we want something we don't have, and thereby we never feel satisfied. Sometimes what is pleasurable in the moment, such as eating a whole pizza, is found to be painful in retrospect.

4. **Repulsion: *Dvesha*.** We have an aversion toward things that have produced unpleasant experiences in the past. We fear repeating them because we want to avoid the possible pain occurring again. Or when we cannot avoid experiences we dislike, we suffer.

5. **Fear of Death: *Abhinivesha*.** When we identify too much with material existence, we stay attached to what is known and fear the unknown. Life becomes predictable, comfortable, and boring.

By working through the kleishas on your path of self-improvement, you can relieve your suffering. The best way to begin is to simply acknowledge them. The following exercises can help you see how they operate and create distress in your life and how you can take steps to work toward change.

1. Ignorance in Your Life (Avidya)

The kleishas cause you to live in a kind of trance state. You may be aware of what's obvious on the surface but unable to recognize the underlying reality. Since this personal spell is fully supported by the beliefs promoted by the society you live in, it's difficult for most of us to recognize we've been hypnotized by the values of popular culture. For example, fashion conditions us to believe that thin is hip and boots are chic.

Avidya can play out on many levels. Although avidya translates to mean "incorrect understanding," it does not necessarily mean stupid or uneducated. On a social scale, if people identify too much with their religion, possessions, status, body, or social class, their ignorance of connectedness with those who are different creates prejudice, intolerance, and racism. If everyone could see that we are all one, there would be no need for hate crimes, discrimination, or war. We would have true equality.

People getting caught up in the illusion that the material reality is all there is leads to rampant greed, resulting in economic injustice and an unequal distribution of wealth. One out of every six Americans lives in poverty, yet the wealthiest 2 percent of all Americans own more wealth than the bottom 95 percent combined. The United States continues to sink deeper and deeper into debt while the dollar drops in value.

Avidya has led to making poor choices about how we handle the earth's resources, resulting in environmental devastation. Animal and plant habitats are lost through our polluting of the environment, endangering species throughout the world. Some believe that by altering ecosystems, we have contributed to climate changes. As a result, we have had severe drought in America, affecting food crops and prices. Wildfires in the west have burned out of control. It is irresponsible to think that our destructive actions don't have consequences.

Those mistaking religious dogma for spirituality justify their fanaticism by creating terrorist acts or by trying to impose their agenda on everyone. Those deluding themselves with the myth of good intentions fight holy wars, but they only create more misery by killing others. Do-gooders may also have well-meaning intentions, but they may wind up lobbying for laws restricting the freedom of others instead of advocating personal responsibility.

On a personal level, if you do not recognize your spiritual nature, it becomes easy to not take responsibility for your life and instead blame others for what happens to you. You begin to believe your negative self-talk, feel like a victim, and beat yourself up. Or you begin to chase after more money you can use to accumulate more things you don't need. You might flaunt or hoard what you have to prove you are okay, but you'll never be satisfied because you never feel you have enough.

My Awakening from Avidya

Years ago while on a spiritual tour to India, I was sitting in the backseat of a cab along with three other members of the group on our way to see the avatar Sai Baba. We were running an hour late, and I was anxious that we wouldn't get to the ashram in time to receive *darshan*, the guru's blessing.

Every day, Sai Baba would make two appearances to his devotees: one in the morning and one in the afternoon. My main reason for coming to India was to see him, because Sai

Baba had appeared to me in a dream a few months prior. He'd held up his right hand toward me, and waves of healing energy had hit me like a lightning bolt. I'd woken up startled and had felt that it was more than a dream. When I received information in the mail two days later about a tour to India that stopped at his ashram, I knew I had to go.

Sai Baba was known for his supernatural powers. He was able to materialize objects with the wave of his hand. Many devotees received gifts of jewelry, mementoes, or *vibhutti* (ashes blessed by him). Others reported that he had the ability to bilocate, meaning he was able to be in two different places at the same time.

While waiting in the cab, I sat feeling sorry for myself as I stared out the window at the palm trees and the open fields. *I spent all this money and traveled so far, and I am going to miss him this morning*, I thought to myself. But at nine thirty, the exact time Sai Baba would have been making his appearance, I felt overcome by an intense emotion. It was as though I was being flooded with light. The feeling was orgasmic and intense. Tears streamed down my face as waves of ecstasy pulsed through me. I was one with everyone and everything in the universe. One of my traveling companions, a seasoned devotee, said nonchalantly, "Oh, you're getting *shaktipat.*"

Shaktipat is an energetic transmission from a spiritual master that awakens the *kundalini*, or life-force energy, of the student. The process dismantles the separation between the ego and one's divine essence. In an instant, the student has a profound glimpse of the spiritual potential that lies dormant within, for the experience propels one into divine union with the soul.

The experience lasted for only a few minutes, but I'll never forget it. For in that moment of moving to higher planes of consciousness, I knew that underneath the world of *maya*, the illusion of the material world, the world of spirit exists. And it is made of love, peace, and bliss.

By the time the cab reached the ashram, it was afternoon. I was feeling back to normal. We walked past tiny shops selling Sai Baba souvenirs, clocks, posters, and buttons that all had a picture of the holy man with his black hair frizzed out into an afro. Thousands of people visited the ashram each day, so when we were ushered to front-row seats my heart nearly went pitter-patter.

I had brought many letters from friends at home asking him for help. I wrote one to him myself, for I was dealing with a difficult personal situation. We sat in the blazing sun for about twenty minutes, and then Sai Baba walked out into the crowd. As he stood in front of me, I smiled and handed him my letters.

I bowed my head and said, "*Namaste*," which translates to mean, "The divine in me greets the divine in you."

The chanting began and lasted for about a half hour or so. And then the show was over. My life had changed forever, for I experienced the spiritual dimension. Finally, after years of practicing yoga and meditation, I had experienced that a greater world exists beyond what the five senses tell us.

You may not have the opportunity to meet with a spiritual master, but using tarot card images can help you begin to break out.

Tarot as a Tool

In many instances, principles in Western occultism and in yogic philosophy overlap. Most people think that tarot cards are used just for fortune telling, but occultists have used tarot cards for centuries to access the ancient knowledge of the kabala, astrology, hermetic magic, and numerology. The twenty-two major arcana represent archetypes that are embedded in the collective consciousness of humanity. The major arcana translate to mean "the greater mysteries," for each card is rich in esoteric symbols designed to help you tap into your inner wisdom.

The Devil tarot card is a perfect symbol for avidya. For this meditation, you'll need a deck of Rider-Waite tarot cards. If you don't have one, search for "the Devil tarot card" online. This card has an image of a devil perched on a block. He has bat wings and goat horns. The pentacle on his head is reversed, symbolizing the false notion that matter can dominate spirit. He sits in darkness, although he holds a lighted torch in his left hand. The monstrous figure is a symbol of man's ignorance of the true nature of reality and his false opinion of his place in the scheme of things.

Beneath him, a naked man and woman are chained to his seat; however, the chains around their necks are so loose they could easily slip off if the man or woman tried to remove them. These figures represent our conscious and subconscious attachments.

In astrology, which is a component part of tarot, the planet Saturn is attributed to this card. Saturn is the planet that brings tests and karmic paybacks. It is associated with restriction and limitation, for it brings structure to your world by helping you know your boundaries, responsibilities, and commitments. Saturn makes you aware of the need for self-control and self-discipline.

The following meditation can help you connect to your inner "devil," to help you discover the shadow areas of your life. This meditation can help reveal your attachments and blocks. Fear not—you will not encounter any outside demonic or evil forces, but you may encounter your previous programming to be afraid. Have your journal and a pen available to write about your experience when you finish.

Devil Card Meditation

Find a comfortable, private place to meditate where you won't be disturbed. For this meditation, you'll need to be surrounded by relaxing music. Give yourself at least half an hour to complete the exercise.

Place the Devil card before you. Focus on it until you can recall it in your mind's eye, and then proceed with the following meditation. You may want to record the words and play it back so that you can be fully in the process.

Begin recording the following script:

Go into a state of relaxation by taking a few deep, connected breaths. Surround yourself in a protective cloak of white light. You are safe and secure.

Imagine the Devil card in your mind's eye growing larger and larger until the figure in it becomes life-size. Step into the card.

The darkness extends out in all directions, yet torchlight burns bright enough for you to see. You are totally safe to experience this.

Do you hear any sounds?

Do you notice any smells?

What do you see?

You notice the devil perched in front of you. He is so grotesque; he is almost like a cartoon. He resembles someone dressed in a Halloween costume. In fact, he looks so strange he appears silly. You begin to laugh at the absurdity. He is as harmless as a stuffed toy.

The devil says in a squeaky voice, "Come here," as he motions for you to take the place of one of the people beneath him. Take note of whether you choose to replace the male or the female. You feel playful, as if you are performing a part in a weird theatrical performance. The figure you replace drops the chain around your neck; it feels heavy, but you can lift it off easily when you want to.

"What are you attached to?" the devil asks.

You are able to see areas of your life that need to be upgraded. You are able to easily know where you need to change. The insights may come as images, words, or feelings.

What do you need to let go of?

Trust what comes.

Once you receive your message, the figure helps you lift the chain off. The devil motions for you to come closer to him. "Here, take this," he says as he hands you the torch.

You feel the warmth of the fire strengthening your vitality. You feel empowered as you hold the light, for you know you always have a choice: to remain in ignorance or to stand in truth.

You take one last look around. You step out of the card. When you do, it shrinks back to its normal size.

End your recording.

Write down your experience in your journal. How did the overall experience feel? Were you afraid to do this exercise because of your religious upbringing?

Describe the environment. Did you hear sounds or notice smells?

What message did you receive? What are your attachments?

Have you been inconsiderate of others, and thereby caused harm or pain? If so, what is the impact on them and yourself?

In what areas of your life do you experience hate? Intolerance? Cruelty? Prejudice?

Are you stuck maintaining appearances at the expense of being authentic?

How can you take yourself less seriously and lighten up? How can you bring more humor and laughter into your life?

Write a positive statement affirming that you can release old ways of being and upgrade your habits.

Baby Steps to Freedom

You free yourself from avidya little by little every time you choose to be conscious in the moment. By practicing yoga *asanas* (poses), you can align your body, mind, and spirit. By sitting quietly in meditation, you can begin to detach from your mind and body and become an observer. In this way, you begin to get to know your authentic self and can start making better choices.

2. Ego in Your Life (Asmita)

When you identify with your personality or body, you become attached to your ego and have a limited perspective. Asmita makes you think you need to be the richest, the smartest, the skinniest ... the list could go on and on. If you think you are your body, then you can easily fall into the trap of not feeling okay about yourself if you are overweight, your teeth are crooked, or you don't live up to fashion model standards. You may think you need to spend thousands of dollars on cosmetic surgery because you feel inadequate. If your self-image runs your life, you are setting yourself up for a struggle as you age and your beauty fades.

When you identify with your personality or ego, you are at the mercy of your emotional responses to circumstances—elated when things go right, and distraught when they don't. You feel like you are on top of the world when you get a promotion, but you are miserable when the company downsizes and you are laid off. Driving your BMW is a thrill, but you are at your wit's end when you discover it's been dented by a hit and run.

When the focus is on the ego, you seek your own interest without concern for others. Instead of acting authentically, the tendency is to want to look good or pretend things are fine when they are not. The ego wants to be right and make others out to be wrong. Your self-expression may be limited because you care too much about what others think and fear being judged or criticized. Or, on the other hand, you may blurt out anything without concern for how your communication will be taken by others.

Even celebrities who seem to have everything are not immune to asmita, for wealth and fame are fleeting. One day you are on top; the next day, you are at the bottom. The news media is always reporting about famous people who have been arrested or are back in rehab struggling with their addictions. Carrie Fisher, who made millions as Princess Leia in *Star Wars* and came from a privileged Hollywood background, is still writing and performing about her struggles with depression in *Wishful Drinking* and *Shockaholic*. Actress Diane Keaton shares in her autobiography, *Then Again*, how she wrestled with bulimia. And in spite of his enormous musical talent and success, Michael Jackson's life tragically ended at an early age.

If you identify with your ego, life doesn't seem fair, for the mind is trapped in duality. Yes, the world is filled with inequities. Some people achieve celebrity status, while others never attain success, no matter how hard they try. But if you can accept that there is a karmic law that is fair and just operating in your life, it can be an empowering context to accept the failures that occur, for karmic lessons drive all of the uncomfortable challenges in your life. Underneath each experience you attract lie your lessons and opportunities for growth.

Exercise:
Transforming Asmita

Physically

There are many New Age therapies that can help you develop a better relationship with your body. Here are a few:

- *Rolfing* is a therapy system created by the Rolf Institute of Structural Integration, founded by Ida Rolfe in 1971. In a series of ten sessions, the body's connective tissues are manipulated in order to release stress patterns and align the spine using gravity.

- The *Feldenkrais Method* helps those who want to reconnect with their natural abilities to move, think, and feel. Private sessions or classes help you be more comfortable performing activities, such as sitting at your computer, playing with your children, or moving with ease.

- *Group motion* or other types of ecstatic dance offer explorations of touch and contact through dance, movement, and voice. Each session includes a guided warm-up and exercises that focus on awareness, improvisation, and somatic intelligence in a safe space.

Ego

You have many roles to play in life; for instance, you may be a mother or father, a teacher or student, an executive or employee. Picture all your clothes hanging in your closet. Imagine that you are an actor and the clothes are costumes for all the personas you play.

- Use a blank sheet in your journal to write down at least ten roles you play in life.
- Since the ego is the "I maker," pay attention to the times you identify with those roles by saying, "I am …"
- Practice detaching from your roles, and observe your actions and responses.

3. Unhealthy Attachment in Your Life (Raga)

Resistance to reality causes suffering. It's easy to get caught up in expectations of how something should be rather than accepting the reality of the moment. So when people and things aren't the way you want them to be, the tendency is to feel upset. If you're emotionally attached to having something a certain way, you're even more miserable when it isn't the way you hoped. This attachment is called raga. But you can choose to remain attached or become detached. It's always up to you.

Here's an example. Frank was returning home from a business trip. He was not a frequent flyer and was unaware that Chicago was notorious for having unpredictable weather in the spring. His flight was scheduled to leave in the late afternoon. When he arrived at the gate, he discovered the flight had been delayed because of a storm. After waiting for over an hour, he learned the flight was canceled. He stood in a long line among other passengers like him, all scrambling to book another flight. By the time he reached the counter, all the later flights had been sold out.

In the past when Frank's flight had been canceled, the airline had put him up in a nearby hotel, so he assumed they would also take care of him now. The airline representative seemed to be unsympathetic to Frank's plight, however, and directed him to customer service. When Frank spoke to the customer service representative, he was told they couldn't help and that he would have to rebook his ticket at the airline counter. When he returned to the airline counter, it was closed.

Upset and hungry, Frank noticed that the only restaurants left open sold fast food. Being on a diet, he couldn't find anything nourishing to eat. This added to his anger and frustration. Spending another night in a hotel wasn't within his budget, so he wound up spending a sleepless night at the airport.

By the time Frank arrived home the next day, he was angry and unpleasant. He snapped at his family, even when they were being loving and supportive. After three days of acting grumpy and withdrawn—making everyone in his house miserable—Frank scheduled a Reiki treatment to help him return to his easygoing self.

After Frank's session, he felt centered and peaceful. But he became aware of how his actions impacted others and felt sorry for how badly he treated his family.

"I was so frustrated because I felt so powerless that I took out my bad mood on my wife and kids," he said with tears in his eyes. "I made my home a living hell. I found fault with everyone. I criticized my wife's cooking after she spent the afternoon preparing my favorite dish, and yelled at my son for playing with his food. I screamed at my teenage daughter for texting at the dinner table," he admitted. "I just spread more bad karma around every chance I could. "

"Well, what are you going to do about it?" I asked.

"I need to apologize and pray they'll forgive me," he said with determination. "And maybe buy my wife some flowers. But I can't continue to get so worked up about things I can't control. Maybe if I learned Reiki, I could use it to detach myself from stressful situations, instead of kicking the dog?"

"Absolutely," I said as I smiled and handed Frank a registration form to an upcoming class.

Exercise:
When Do You Become Attached?

Here are some other modern-day situations that may cause you to become distressed:

- Your favorite television series ends or is preempted by a political speech.
- Your love interest doesn't call.

- The morning coffee isn't available.
- The neighborhood restaurant sells out of your favorite entrée just as you're ready to order.
- Your Internet service is down.
- Your computer crashes or locks up.
- Your spouse is in a bad mood.
- All of the convenient parking spaces are taken.
- Your vacation is rained out.
- Your boss criticizes your performance.
- Your train is delayed, or your flight home is canceled.
- Your appointment is late.
- Your car gets a flat tire.
- Your cell phone battery dies when you're expecting an important call.

Make a list of past situations in which you resisted what was happening because you thought it should be different; in other words, list events in your life that didn't occur the way you expected. Now observe your list. What types of situations cause you to respond by becoming upset? Do you notice a pattern?

Practicing Detachment

When things go wrong, the universe is not conspiring against you. Computers, cars, and appliances wear out or break. Nature doesn't always cooperate with your plans: picnics are rained out, and traveling doesn't always go smoothly. It's natural to want to invent an explanation in your mind when unexpected circumstances arise. You might be surprised to hear that some people think getting a flat tire means they are under a black magic spell!

The trick to handling situations when things go wrong is to not take it personally. Wallowing in emotional upset just wastes time and energy. Instead, take a deep breath. Take a moment to experience the frustration or inconvenience of your situation. Allow yourself to feel anger, sadness, fear, or even a moment of helplessness. Then let the feelings go. When we truly experience and acknowledge our emotions, they often disappear.

Trying to invent an explanation is pointless. Fabricating a story that may or may not be true will only cause more upset and anxiety. The person who cuts you off in traffic is indeed arrogant or reckless or both, but it's not a personal affront directed toward you. Step back and observe the situation as if you were watching it on a movie screen. Accept the reality of your circumstance. Surrender to the process. Simply acknowledge that what is happening is occurring despite the fact that you'd prefer it to be different. Give up thinking it should be another way, and accept the way that it is.

Then take a deep breath and ask yourself if there are any actions you need to take to resolve your situation. What is the first step? Once you identify what you need to do, you will have clarity about how to proceed.

Practicing emotional detachment empowers you to stop being a victim of circumstance and take action to transform the situation. When you detach from the negativity in your life, you have more time and energy to do things you enjoy.

4. Repulsion in Your Life (Dvesha)

Dvesha is the opposite of raga, for it is when we reject things. Once you've had a difficult experience, it's natural to fear that it will repeat itself. You may even unconsciously avoid new experiences that remind you of that past experience, assuming they will bring you similar pain.

There's an old saying that if you fall off your horse, you should get back in the saddle and continue riding. This will prevent you from anticipating another fall. Facing fears directly is the only way to overcome them. If you don't get right back on that horse, your fears will escalate and it will become only harder to continue.

Here's an example of how fear can stop you if you let it. Unless you're a thrill seeker, you probably don't want to feel that your life is in danger while on vacation. My husband and I were spending time on a lovely remote island off the coast of Mexico. We spent a glorious week floating in turquoise water, reading in swaying hammocks, combing the beach for seashells, and eating the catch of the day at local restaurants. It was so romantic to take moonlit walks under a sky full of stars and sip fruit juice at the pool. We were sad when it was time to leave.

We needed to take a water taxi across fifteen miles of lagoon back to the mainland to catch our flight home. It was sunny the morning of our departure, but the wind was blowing about twenty knots, which made the water much rougher than it had been on our trip over. When we arrived at the dock, we noticed that a Canadian couple who were also to take the water taxi donned life jackets. I thought this was odd, as I noticed that none had been provided by the taxi service. We loaded our luggage into the twenty-foot open launch and set off toward land. As the boat sped out into the open water, the wind kicked up. The boat repeatedly stood up at a forty-five-degree angle and then slammed down over the waves. Being tossed in this dramatic up-and-down motion reminded me of riding a mechanical bull in a Texas bar, except that no one was cheering us on and I wouldn't be handed a margarita when the ride was over.

I closed my eyes and began to chant mantras (repetitive words that are a kind of prayer) to give myself something to focus on; otherwise, I would have been screaming at the top of my lungs.

When we were about halfway across the lagoon, we stopped being able to move forward at all because the wind was blowing so hard against us. The driver cut the motor, making the boat sway from side to side at a sixty-five-degree angle. Not being a great swimmer, I was terrified we'd capsize; I doubted I could dog-paddle the seven miles needed to reach the shore. Our companions were shrieking and soaked with spray, but my husband, who had spent years sailing, wasn't the least bit fazed. The driver wasn't concerned either, except for the fact that, perhaps, he wouldn't get a big tip.

The driver moved our bags to the front of the boat to redistribute the weight, and we sped off again. Somehow that made all the difference, and we safely reached shore. As I stepped on solid ground, my hands were shaking, my knees were wobbling, and I had a bad case of dry mouth.

Both before that incident and since, there have been no reports of boats capsizing offshore the Mexican Riviera, but when my husband asked about planning our next spring vacation, my automatic response was to suggest we try going somewhere new. Even though we'd had a fabulous time on the rest of our trip in Mexico, I had to make a huge effort not to allow that one unpleasant memory to influence my decision to return. To do so, I used the meditation in the next exercise to check in with myself and get back in the saddle. When we returned to the island the following spring, I was thrilled to see that the water taxis provided life jackets.

Exercise: Getting Back on the Horse

Before doing the meditation that follows, use the lists below as a springboard to help you determine areas of your life that you have been avoiding because of fear caused by a previous bad experience. Also note that if you are hanging onto old resentments, sadness, or anger along with the fear, it will block you from moving forward.

In the area of relationships:

- Do you say you want a relationship, yet you make no effort to date?
- Do you always pick partners who are unavailable?

- Instead of reaching out, do you expect others to contact you?
- Do you complain that you never meet anyone interesting?

In the area of work:

- Do you hate your job but resist looking for something better?
- Are you underpaid, yet fear asking for a raise?
- Do you feel that you're wasting your potential, yet avoid researching other options?
- Do you fear being rejected?

In the area of health and well-being:

- Do you hold back instead of expressing yourself?
- Are you unhappy with your weight and state of health?
- Are you trapped in scarcity, unable to fully experience the abundance your life holds?
- Are you in debt?
- Do you take unnecessary physical risks?

Now make a list of the areas in your life that you feel you have been avoiding because of past experiences. Pick one item from that list to work with in the meditation.

Back-in-the-Saddle Meditation
The intention of this meditation is to address an area of your life that is blocked. You can practice this meditation

as many times as you need to explore as many stuck areas as you'd like.

Be sure to take a couple of minutes to pause after each question in the meditation to allow enough time for your inner guidance to come through and help you answer. The whole process should take about twenty minutes.

You may want to record this meditation ahead of time while playing soothing music in the background so that you can be fully in the process.

Begin recording the following script:

Relax into a comfortable position and close your eyes. Practice breathing consciously for twenty breaths. When you feel at peace and centered, select one area of your life in which you stopped participating because you were hurt in the past and fear being hurt again.

Where do you feel the fear in your body?

Does it feel spread out everywhere, or is it concentrated in one spot?

What color is it? Give it a definite shape.

Now imagine that you can just slip this colored shape off your body for a moment in the same way you'd shed a piece of clothing. Envision it outside your body, sitting next to you. Allow yourself to experience how it feels to be free from it.

Does this fear belong to you? Or have you taken it from someone else? Your parents? A friend? Your spouse? If it is from some other person, imagine it floating up and away, dissolving into the white light of universal love. If it belongs to you, continue.

Now look inside your heart to see how you feel about your issue. Is there another emotion connected to this fear? Is it sadness? Anger? Resentment?

Is there someone you need to forgive? Do you need to forgive yourself?

Is there something you need to say to resolve this emotion? What do you need to say to anyone else involved in this fear so that you can be free? Say it without holding back. Speak it, even though it may not be "nice." Breathe into it the emotion you feel and allow it to release.

Fear is the opposite of love. What would you do without this fear? What would you want to do if this fear weren't coloring your decisions?

Check in to see if you are truly ready to let it go. Know that the fear is not who you are. You are bigger than your fear. If you no longer need this fear, let it return to wherever it came from. Have it dissolve into space.

Imagine a white light entering the top of your head. Feel it moving down your face, down your chest and torso. Then feel the light filling your heart with love, bathing every cell of your body in healing energy. Fill yourself with the light of your own creative essence.

In just a few moments, you will count from one up to five. On the count of five you'll be wide awake, totally refreshed, and feeling good.

One … two … three … four … five. Open your eyes. You are wide awake. Wide awake.

End your recording.

Now take as much time as you need to write down any impressions, feelings, or body sensations you had during the meditation and any words of guidance that came to you.

Knowing Your Limits

Another factor that influences your choices is the tendency to reject new types of experiences, even though you have no history with them. We all do this. Although you may be open to many new experiences, there are some types of experiences you wouldn't dare try. For example, I like to think of myself as an adventurous person, having traveled around the globe in search of new experiences. I've climbed mountains, kayaked in the Pacific, hiked up Cathedral Rock in Sedona, Arizona, and snorkeled in the Caribbean. However, there are certain experiences that just don't appeal to me. In fact, you couldn't pay me to have them.

Of the top two experiences that I'll be sure to avoid, the first is skydiving. My friend Barbara, who is in her fifties, was raving about how exciting it is to jump out of an airplane while cruising somewhere between ten and thirteen thousand feet. She finds it exhilarating to take a big step out into space and free-fall for up to seventy-five seconds before her parachute opens, allowing her to soar like an eagle for up to nine minutes. She has done it over thirty times.

The second on my list of experiences to avoid is swimming with sharks. A client once shared how she sailed from San Francisco to the Farallon Islands to dive with great white sharks, all to overcome her fear of deep water. Equipped with scuba gear and a wetsuit, she was lowered into the icy, murky ocean in a cage so she could experience twenty-foot-long sharks swimming around her like giant limousines.

Exercise:
Knowing Your Range

Just for fun, you might make a list of such experiences or adventures that you want to avoid. Remember, these are experiences with which you have no prior history; they just don't appeal to you. Next list some experiences you do want to have and are not afraid to pursue. What have you always dreamed of doing? If money weren't a factor in your ability to do it, what adventures would you embark upon? What did you fantasize about doing as a child? Now compare your two lists. What is your range between something you never want to do and something you crave?

5. Death in Your Life (Abhinivesha)

The fear of death, abhinivesha, is the last kleisha (distorted view of reality). Death is an inevitable reality. While conducting past-life regression workshops over the years, I've met many people whose fear of death is due to their religious programming. During the workshops, people have reported they were taught that they would burn in hell for eternity because they got divorced, told a lie, or ate meat on Friday. Another reported that her parents told her if she were good she would "sit next to God for eternity." She said that she thought this boredom would be a type of hell to endure.

Those who were raised without religion said they'd simply cease to exist after death; it would be like falling into a dreamless sleep and never awakening. Most people reported feeling unprepared for their eventual death and uncomfortable just thinking about it.

If you believe in reincarnation, it is easier to accept death —for if you've lived before, you've died before. Like the yogis, Buddhists, and pagans, you see life and death as a continuous cycle of change and renewal. Past-life exploration helps you connect with your soul, the part of you that is eternal and divine, and see that it has survived. The personality and the body changes from lifetime to lifetime, but the soul stays constant.

I have helped many people conquer their fear of death by guiding them to their past lives. During the regression, one sees life in a bigger perspective while in a trance-state. This brings about a sense of peace, love, and comfort and an understanding that each life has its lessons. One sometimes learns that relationships in this life have ties in other lifetimes, affirming that we are also connected to others throughout time by our love—for love never dies.

My work as a medium has also helped people connect with loved ones who have died. It is especially hard to deal with the grief and loss when one has lost someone suddenly through an accident or unexpectedly. Most clients want to know that their loved one is all right. When one connects to loved ones on the other side by receiving a message that is very personal, it brings comfort to the bereaved.

Sometimes people have unresolved issues with those who have passed away. Being able to have a conversation with those who are deceased can bring forgiveness, understanding, and healing for both parties.

Exercise:
Releasing Abhinivesha

Play Dead

Practicing the yoga asana *corpse pose (savasana)* can help you gradually release your fear of death, for you learn how to detach from your body, thoughts, and emotions. In learning how to let go of your ego, you can begin to connect with everyone and everything in the universe and experience oneness. Continued practice will also relax your nervous system and rejuvenate your body, mind, and spirit.

1. Lie on your back with your knees bent and your feet on the floor.

2. Extend one leg out at a time, bringing your feet together, toes pointing toward the ceiling.

3. Release your legs so they flop out away from each other.

4. Bring your arms alongside your body, palms facing up. Allow space around your arms.

5. Focus on your breath as you begin to relax.

6. Totally let go of any tension in your body.

7. Allow your eyes to drop back into their sockets.

8. Release your tongue. Keep letting go.

9. Stay in this position for five minutes.

Afterward, bend your arms and legs and roll onto your right side. When you are ready, sit back up and notice the effects.

Explore Your Past Lives

My book *Karmic Healing: Clearing Past-Life Blocks to Present-Day Love, Health, and Happiness* gives meditations and tools for discovering your past lives and how they affect your present.

Getting a past-life regression with a reputable therapist or healer in your area can also be a life-changing experience.

Have a Reading with a Medium

A reading can help you to know that your deceased loved ones are well and are still with you. Knowing they are watching over you can bring comfort, for you can experience that you are not alone. If you have unfinished business—something not said or heard—with your loved ones, a reading can bring closure, which allows you to gain peace of mind.

Unraveling Distorted Perceptions (Kleishas)

Now that you have begun to untangle the kleishas, the veil to your authentic self has begun to lift—you will see the world and yourself more clearly now that you aren't seeing with a distorted view. Every time you work at dissolving the veil, you will gain new insights and new perceptions. You will begin to replace suffering with peace of mind. But be patient, for what took a lifetime to develop takes time to unravel.

Chapter Three

CHOOSE GROWTH

Now that we've recognized how our ability to make choices is colored by past experiences and misperceptions, we are ready to move on to learning about karmic patterns. A karmic pattern is composed of repetitive actions we've made in the past combined with automatic choices we make in the present.

In this chapter, you'll learn all the components that make up a karmic pattern and how to determine when one is in operation. Then focusing on the three main areas of your life—relationships, work, and well-being—you'll discover how to use the three-step Karmic Pattern Formula (clarify, clear, and create) to transform any areas that feel blocked or stuck, and to make choices freed from the limitations of the past.

Choosing Trust

When Karen came into my office for a tarot card reading, her main concern was, "Am I ever going to meet someone special?" Even though she appeared to be staring at the red clay-fired Aztec mask of death and rebirth hanging on my salmon-colored walls, I could tell she was lost in her thoughts. She nervously shifted from side to side as she shuffled the well-worn tarot deck into three piles. I asked her to carefully choose ten cards without looking at the pictures.

First, for the position representing the heart of the problem, Karen pulled the Hermit card, which suggested that she felt isolated and lonely.

"I never meet anyone interesting," she grumbled as, next, she selected an image of a heart being pierced by three swords. "Everyone in the city is so unfriendly."

Perhaps she was looking outside herself for the source of her trouble, so she felt helpless and powerless to change her circumstances. I could tell she was ready to release self-sabotaging patterns.

The Lovers card lay in the position representing a past relationship. Karen told me it had been five years since she'd broken up with her last boyfriend. It had ended badly, as he'd cheated on her.

"I don't know if I can ever trust someone again," she admitted. "I was devastated."

The Eight of Pentacles signified the recent past.

Next, the image of a man hammering away at his workbench prompted me to ask Karen if she spent a lot of time at her job.

"All I do is work," she said. "By the time I get home, I'm too tired to do anything but watch television. But I'm so bored. I need to get a life."

The next position represented the key to her success. Karen selected the Sun card. The picture of a smiling child with his arms outstretched, riding a white horse, symbolized her need to be playful and connect with her inner child.

"Gee, Karen, what *do* you do for fun?" I asked her, intuiting she'd become a workaholic to escape being with her feelings.

She replied, with tears in her eyes, "I used to be very active. I loved to go rollerblading, hiking, and bicycling. But now I've turned into a couch potato."

The next card was the healing angel of Temperance.

Being empathetic, I could feel how Karen's grief was weighing her down, so I asked her, "Is it possible you don't have a personal life because you've avoided dealing with your anger and grief?"

Karen nodded her head in reply.

"Are you ready to forgive your ex and move on?" I asked.

"Yes, it's time." Karen's worried expression faded, and color flushed her cheeks.

When I asked her if she could take responsibility for her role in the relationship, she replied, "The truth is, he wasn't right for me, yet I couldn't leave him."

"Well, there you have it, Karen. You are not a victim," I said, smiling as I watched her slough off the pain of that old karmic pattern. Karen's face softened, and she looked ten years younger.

I probed Karen to look deeper into herself. "What is the spiritual lesson you need to learn from this?"

"I need to trust myself," she replied confidently. "Even when things don't work out as planned, it's all for the best."

I asked Karen to write down a few of her favorite pleasures. As she made her list, a weight seemed to lift from her shoulders. I then asked her to schedule three of her pleasures in her calendar. She committed to joining Match.com, setting up a Facebook page, and enrolling in a bicycle club by the end of the week.

The final tarot card, in the outcome position, was the Knight of Wands, which I interpreted as her need to take action in order to have adventure and fun.

"Have you reached out to others at all?" I asked her. "Do you call new acquaintances to just check in, to see how they're doing, or to go out for coffee?"

"No, I just wait for them to call me," she seemed embarrassed to admit.

In answering the question, Karen realized that it was actually she who was being cold and unfriendly, and not others. By shifting her point of view in this way, she saw that she needed to extend herself to people and learn to be open and sociable.

Karen left the office with a sparkle in her eye, obviously feeling confident with a renewed view of her life—a view in which she could stop blaming the city for its lack of available men and start accepting responsibility for her personal situation.

Six months later, she called to say she was in a committed relationship with the man of her dreams.

The Karmic Pattern Formula

Since you are always in action, you are always in the process of sowing seeds of new karma and reaping rewards or consequences from either what you've done or what you haven't done in the past.

Now let's return to study the anatomy of a karmic pattern and learn how to recognize the signs that it's operating in your life. I call repetitive complaining and blaming, combined with a lack of power to change an ongoing, unsatisfying situation, a *karmic pattern*. In other words, a pattern is karmic when it's composed of repetitive actions (karma) combined with choices made without conscious thought.

When a karmic pattern is active in you, you have a tendency to feel like a victim. Your point of view is usually one of struggle and of feeling separate and alone. Sometimes you also hold a false assumption about the ways things *should* be.

However, the situations in which karmic patterns prevail provide you with opportunities to learn about yourself. Once these patterns are identified, you can upgrade your behavior, choosing new ways to conduct yourself and becoming clear on the actions you need to take, all of which will transform your life.

The Karmic Pattern Formula outlined below can help you with this process, leading you to discover when a karmic pattern is in operation, identify its component parts, and then dismantle it. Ultimately, this three-step formula enables you to transform areas of your life that aren't working.

1. **Clarify.** Becoming aware that a situation is repeating, and recalling its roots, is the first step to releasing it.

2. **Clear.** Understanding the spiritual lesson attached to the karmic pattern frees you to rewrite the script for the life you want.

3. **Create.** Committing to take a specific action that works for the highest good of all helps you upgrade your behavior and unleash your passion.

When you take responsibility for recognizing your karmic patterns, you begin to take control of your life. When you take control of your life, you demonstrate power. Power is the capacity to produce results, manifest your intentions, and live your dreams.

1. Clarify: Locating and Examining a Karmic Pattern

Blaming and Complaining

You have to locate a karmic pattern before you can change it. You may find karmic patterns in your relationships, finances, or ability to express yourself. Identifying a karmic pattern is perhaps the most difficult step because one of its symptoms is blaming and complaining, which cover up your lack of responsibility in the matter.

Karen's constant complaint was, "I never meet anyone interesting," and she blamed the city for its lack of available men. She was unaware that she was the one who set her life up this way. Her job didn't offer any opportunities to meet an available partner, yet she worked overtime, leaving no space in her schedule for her personal life. She hadn't joined a dating service, and her social life was nil, yet she wondered why she was lonely.

Also, ever since her ex had cheated on her five years before, she'd been feeling like a victim, another symptom of a karmic pattern. Instead of taking responsibility for her role in the breakup, she wallowed in self-pity for being dumped. She fantasized about Prince Charming appearing out of nowhere and knocking on her door, rather than taking practical steps to make herself available. She was frustrated and unhappy, but she was unaware that she'd lost her power to change her situation.

Karen also didn't know she held false assumptions about her social life, another indicator of a karmic pattern. Once she uncovered her mistaken expectation that people would call, however, she was free to become more proactive in pursuing a satisfying social life. So instead of waiting for others to call her, and then being disappointed if they didn't, she made the conscious effort to connect with others.

Once Karen shifted her view of herself as victim to one of being the responsible party, she was able to reclaim her power and take control of her situation. She saw that she was in charge of the condition of her social life and that the lesson she was to learn was to trust herself. It was up to her to create meaningful relationships, but her current choice of nonaction wasn't producing good results. So she discovered new actions she needed to take to create a satisfying personal life.

Your Point of View

How you choose to view what happens to you affects whether you experience struggle or ease in all areas of life. During every challenge you encounter, you are either living within an empowering context or are lacking power. If you do not hold yourself accountable for choosing your point of view as you deal with everyday trials, the tendency is to blame your misfortune or unpleasant circumstances on someone else. For instance, if your mate cheats on you, it would be easy to automatically fault him for being unfaithful and criticize him for being untrustworthy. You could fall into the trap of being a victim, becoming bitter, and closing your heart off to loving another person.

But blaming is detrimental, because you are abdicating your responsibility and giving away your power. A more constructive approach would be to face the problems directly. See the part that you played in the situation, and be accountable for your role in the matter. Remember, every time you point at someone, three of your fingers are pointing back at you.

Many people unconsciously use blaming as a defense mechanism. Rather than deal with the truth about one's own shortcomings, it's easier to accuse others of having a negative quality or trait. For example, a client of mine named Jules referred to his father as a narcissistic tyrant. All his life, Jules blamed his father—who was a self-centered alpha type—for his own lack of success. But during his reading with me, Jules discovered that the real problem stemmed from the fact that he'd never stood up to his father. He learned early in life that it was impossible to successfully confront his father on anything, and he believed that would never change.

Jules also saw that his fear of confrontation had seeped into all areas of his life. He took on the nice-guy role, which left him feeling exploited and powerless most of the time. Once Jules realized this, he was empowered to change how he related to others and was able to be more direct. Those who couldn't accept his honesty and newfound self-esteem left his life, but Jules was able to form new relationships with those who were able to take responsibility for their actions, and thereby he felt more fulfilled.

Blaming keeps you stuck in a small or limited point of view that doesn't serve your highest good.

Assumptions

Assumptions can also be part of a karmic pattern. Assumptions are beliefs or ideas that you hold to be facts, yet they may or may not be true. You make assumptions every day. For example, when you cross the street at a traffic light, you assume that drivers will obey the traffic laws and stop for you. And most of the time they do.

However, often you make assumptions that are not so obvious; you make assumptions about people and situations that stem from the way you see the world. That unique view is shaped by your beliefs, opinions, and attitudes toward particular subjects. Your gender, race, economic class, and religious values also influence how you see the world. A white male born in an upper-class Republican family in Texas probably views the world differently from a Native American woman born on a reservation. A devout Catholic's view of the world is not the same as a Buddhist's, and someone who has traveled the world has a different perspective from someone who has never left his hometown.

It's easy to assume that others agree with your world views. But because we think our assumptions are truths that everyone shares, often these assumptions bring pain. Take Bonnie, for instance.

Assuming People Are Thoughtful

After a long discussion with her spouse, Bonnie invited her husband's sister and two teenage nieces to spend Christmas weekend at their home. Bonnie worked full time as a social worker, so she didn't have a lot of time to prepare for the holidays. Her husband never helped with cooking or decorating, so she knew she'd have to do it herself.

With Christmas less than a month away, Bonnie spent her evenings trimming the banister with pine roping and red velvet ribbons. She enjoyed stringing lights around the huge picture window and loved hanging the antique glass ornaments she had inherited on her perfectly shaped twelve-foot Douglas fir.

But by mid-December, Bonnie's back ached and her feet hurt from standing in long checkout lines at the grocery store and mall. And she was tired. Every night for the past three weeks, she had stayed up hours after her usual bedtime trying to get everything done. Night after night, Bonnie had carefully wrapped gifts with sparkling paper and silk ribbons and placed them under the tree. She had put clean sheets on the beds in the guest rooms and folded fluffy new towels for the bathrooms.

Then early on the morning of Christmas Eve, the day her guests were to arrive, Bonnie began preparing their Christmas Eve dinner. She spent hours in the kitchen, peeling shrimp for appetizers, stuffing the turkey, roasting vegetables, and baking gingerbread cookies.

When her guests arrived for dinner, Bonnie's Victorian house looked like it could have been from a picture in *The Night Before Christmas*. The lights twinkled, emanating a warm glow. Red embroidered stockings hung from the mantle, and a fire crackled in the fireplace. Champagne chilled in an ice bucket and fluted crystal goblets sparkled on the table, which was set with fine linen and china. The house smelled of pine, cinnamon, and ginger.

After their delicious meal, a sumptuous feast, Bonnie was surprised when no one offered to help her clear the table. She had assumed that her guests would pitch in and at least take some of the plates from the dining room into the kitchen. Instead, her husband and guests retired to the living room to savor their hot buttered rum in front of the fire.

Bonnie was still cleaning the kitchen when everyone else announced they were going to bed.

Maybe they're all just tired from their trip, Bonnie thought. *Tomorrow will be different. I'm sure they'll want to help me prepare dinner.*

But Bonnie thought wrong. Her sister-in-law spent the entire day reading in her room, only coming downstairs for coffee, while her husband and the girls went to a movie.

That night, Bonnie was left alone to slave in the kitchen and prepare another five-course meal. And once again, no one offered to clear the table, load the dishwasher, or hand-wash the crystal goblets. Bonnie was hurt and angry. She felt like a maid, yet she didn't want to say anything for fear of being rude.

By the time Monday came, Bonnie was in tears. As her husband was driving their guests to the airport, she looked through the guest rooms and bathrooms and thought, *They didn't even offer to bring the sheets to the laundry room. The bathrooms are a complete mess, and they didn't cook or help me at all. I can't believe how inconsiderate people can be.*

When Bonnie told her story to me a week later, she began to regain her sense of humor. Being able to talk about her experience gave her relief.

"I've been so angry at myself this past week for being a doormat. I thought that because I'm a thoughtful person, other people would be as well. Boy, was I wrong." Bonnie smiled as she gained a new perspective on what happened over the holiday.

"Just because you have good manners doesn't mean other people do," I chimed in. "What did you learn from this experience?"

"Once I saw they weren't going to pitch in, I could have asked for help. I wasn't being authentic because I withheld what I wanted. Communicating works better than assuming."

Exercise:
Step One: Clarify—
Identifying Unwanted Conditions

This exercise will help you to discover how karmic patterns are operating in your life. The first step in the Karmic Pattern Formula—to **clarify**—will enable you to become aware that a situation is repetitive and then to recall its roots.

Start by titling a new page in your journal "Unwanted Conditions." Under this title, take a few minutes to write down areas of your life that aren't working as well as you'd like. Examine all areas of your life—your body, finances, communication, family, home, relationships, creativity, work, health, sex, career, social concerns, and love life are just a few.

Next to each problem area you write down, note how long it has been a problem, and then think about how often you see yourself doing the following:

- feeling at a loss for power or feeling victimized
- complaining
- blaming others for your situation

- expecting something from someone and being disappointed when you don't get it
- making assumptions rather than communicating
- being irresponsible
- feeling overwhelmed or anxious
- holding stress and tension in your body
- developing an illness
- having an injury

Write down any insights you have in these areas. Be sure to save this list for later, as you will use it in the next section and at the end of this chapter to clear your karmic patterns.

Don't worry. Circumstances that allow your karmic patterns to surface happen for a reason; they allow your patterns to rise to your awareness so that you can eventually release them. If you didn't have problems to challenge you, your life would stagnate. You'd feel comfortable, but you'd also become very bored. So as you go through this process, remember that each event you encounter offers you the chance to not only gain insight about yourself but also to attain your deepest desires.

2. Clear—Identifying Your Spiritual Lessons

Spiritual Lessons

A positive component of a karmic pattern is the opportunity for growth. Anytime we transform ignorance into wisdom or upgrade our behavior, we develop personally; the more we learn from our mistakes, the wiser we become. One who has gleaned wisdom from life's challenges usually has gained strength of character. Character defines who we are inside, which, in turn, affects our choices.

Because of this process, the Karmic Pattern Formula can make you aware that life is a learning experience, so that every challenge you encounter becomes an opportunity for your personal expansion and evolution.

If you watch closely, you can even see the *clearing* part of the Karmic Pattern Formula play out in television programs. For example, some say popular courtroom reality shows are exploitive—viewers only watch them to feel better about their own lives when compared to the lives of the litigants. But back in the eighties, while I was staying at an ashram in New York, I discovered that these TV programs were a great way to learn about karma.

After a late lunch of vegetable curry and a few rounds of chanting mantras, I was scheduled to have a private meeting with my guru. As I knocked on his office door, my palms were sweaty and my mouth was dry. I was nervous to be in the presence of one who seemed to possess all the secrets of the universe. He had left a successful career as a brain surgeon to become a Sanskrit scholar and an accomplished author of books about the philosophy of yoga.

When I entered the room, my beloved teacher, a small-statured man with cinnamon-colored skin and a long, gray, scraggly beard, sat with his legs folded in the lotus position on a cushion on the floor. He wore a saffron-colored robe and a *mala* made of *rudraksha* beads wrapped around his wrist. He smelled of sandalwood. I was not expecting to find him half hypnotized, staring intently into a portable nineteen-inch television. He was watching a man stupidly admit to being a deadbeat dad on *The People's Court.*

I asked the inevitable question. "Guru-ji, why are you watching that?"

"I'm learning about Americans," he said with a big grin. "It's all about karma."

I'll never know whether this scenario was totally staged, to teach me about karma, or if it was a glimpse of a spiritual master's humanity, but from that moment on I was hooked on courtroom television. Even Judge Judy, who has over twenty-four years of family court experience, believes that her TV show helps people, as she uses her skills and wisdom to influence millions every day.

These reality courtroom episodes perfectly illustrate that, throughout life, you have the opportunity to grow wise through experience. In every show, someone is in a jam, usually from having made a bad choice. People get into disputes about all sorts of things, ranging from damaged property to infidelity.

A common problem people have is loaning money to lovers who never pay them back. After hearing both sides of the story in these cases, the judge usually says, "You should have known better. Why would you think he'd pay you back when he doesn't even have a job? You didn't have a written contract, so he doesn't owe you anything."

And in that moment, the plaintiff in each of these cases usually has an epiphany or an aha moment. She realizes she made a bad decision by trusting someone who wasn't trustworthy and will pay for that mistake by losing the case. At the end of the case, the plaintiff is interviewed and usually says something to the effect of, "I'll be more careful about loaning money in the future."

Over the years, I've performed many healing sessions for people who have suffered from making bad choices. In each session, I point out that in spite of the pain and hurt, there is always a gift: our experiences teach us and help us grow. And what we gain is precious wisdom.

Wisdom is defined as the knowledge to make sound decisions and practice good judgment. Ultimately, if you recognize your challenges as opportunities to grow, you can gain wisdom from meeting these challenges and learning from them. In doing so, life becomes an extraordinary adventure.

I call the wisdom gleaned from opportunity *spiritual lessons.* Connecting with your spiritual lesson is like having an "aha—I've got it!" moment. Some call it a moment of breaking through confusion to understanding. It is a moment in which you realize that you have intuitively known your spiritual lesson all along but have been resistant to really owning it. In that moment the lesson becomes suddenly clear, because your resistance unexpectedly dissolves in a flash, as with a strike of lightning.

Standing Up for Yourself

Carol's constant complaint was, "My back hurts so bad, I can hardly walk." She blamed her ailing health for her misery.

Carol was in the advertising business and worked long hours, seven days a week. For years, her employer never seemed to appreciate her hard work, so Carol felt ever compelled to do more and more. Now her life didn't seem like her own. The last time she'd had a vacation was a few months prior to our visit, when she'd taken off time because she'd had the flu.

Carol had been getting medical tests, blood work, and MRIs to uncover the source of her back pain, but doctors had told her to seek out holistic alternatives because they could find nothing medically wrong.

As it turned out, here was the problem: Carol had been living a stressful lifestyle for five years, and her health was beginning to break down. In addition to the stress of being overworked and feeling underappreciated, Carol felt no one at work listened to her. After years of having her ideas passed over at meetings, she had learned to keep her mouth shut. Her teeth were clenched and her jaw ached because she couldn't express herself, so, not surprisingly, she also suffered from temporomandibular joint disorder (TMJ). It was as if her words had backed up in her throat, making it feel as though there were a steel trap inside her jaw.

By the time Carol called me for an appointment, she was in excruciating pain but was unaware that she had a karmic pattern. During her session, I pointed out that one's body, mind, and spirit are holistically interconnected. Carol could understand when I told her that her body was sending her the message that work was hurting her. She said she knew that she couldn't keep going at this pace, but she didn't know how else she could make a living if she quit. She hadn't even had any time to think her life could be any other way.

Trying to empower Carol to take responsibility for her actions, I asked, "Why are you doing this to yourself?"

Carol burst into tears. "I just wanted my boss to see what a great job I'm doing, but instead, I've allowed him to take advantage of me. It's like I'm invisible. I sacrifice my needs for everyone else. I work longer hours but don't get paid for overtime."

"What do you need to do to heal?" I asked.

Carol then had an aha moment. "I need to stand up for myself!" she said, jumping out of her chair.

Carol had thought that her physical health was the cause of her pain, when actually it was her emotional well-being that was the source of the problem. Her complaint was her aching back, but her problem stemmed from her stressful lifestyle. When Carol shifted her point of view of herself from that of victim to responsible adult, she saw that her health issues were occurring because she hadn't learned how to take care of her emotional needs. And then, after being silent for so long, she saw that her associated spiritual lesson was to speak up for herself.

Exercise:
Step Two: Clear—
Identifying Your Spiritual Lessons

The second step of the Karmic Pattern Formula is to **clear**—
to understand the spiritual lesson attached to the karmic
pattern you have. This step frees you to rewrite the script
for the rest of your life.

To take this second step, go to the "Unwanted Conditions" page in your journal, where you've listed areas in your
life that aren't working as well as you'd like. You've noted
how long they have been a problem and have become mindful about those situations in which the symptoms manifest.

You've also, in the previous section, recognized the
symptoms of a karmic pattern:

- being irresponsible

- feeling at a loss for power or feeling victimized

- complaining

- blaming others for your situation

- expecting something from someone and being disappointed when you don't get it

- making assumptions rather than communicating

- feeling overwhelmed or anxious

- holding stress and tension in your body

- developing an illness

- having an injury

Now pick one item from your list of unwanted conditions and use it as the title on a new blank page. Then write responses to the following questions and comments:

1. Are you playing a victim role in this situation in your life?

2. Reclaim your power by changing your point of view of yourself from that of victim to that of responsible party. Think about how you can take total responsibility for your part in the situation.

3. Commit to stop blaming and complaining.

4. Do you have an assumption about this area in your life?

5. What are you not communicating that needs to be said?

6. Notice where you are holding stress related to this pattern in your body.

7. Whether you prefer gentle stretching or a physically demanding aerobics session, there are a variety of ways to release stress from your body. Some people prefer to work out alone at home using a DVD or to jog in solitude. Others would rather move with a group in a dance class or play a sport, such as tennis or racquetball, with a partner. Any activity that accelerates your heart rate can also relieve tension.

Disciplines like yoga or tai chi can harmonize body, mind, and spirit, and help you develop core strength and flexibility. The breathing exercises used in these practices also aid in relaxation and the ability to concentrate.

Other ways of relieving tension from the body are spa treatments, such as massage, acupuncture, reflexology, therapeutic facials, salt baths, saunas, hot tubs, or Reiki.

Which will you choose to help you release your karmic pattern from your body?

1. If you have an illness or injury, note how it's affecting you.

2. What behavior or old way of being do you need to let go of?

3. What is your spiritual lesson? What quality do you need to develop? What do you need to learn?

Finally, write down all your other thoughts and insights, but leave some space at the end of the page for the final step of the formula.

3. Create: Uncovering New Actions

When you're living with a karmic pattern, it's easy to feel resigned. It becomes easy to take on the attitude of "been there, done that," so that life seems stale, leaving no room for surprises. Once you clarify and clear a karmic pattern, however, a newfound freedom to create the rest of your life emerges. There is excitement when you let go of the expectations of the past and become childlike again, full of curiosity and wonder. Each moment becomes fresh and new. Like an artist standing in front of a blank canvas, you enter an unknown world and explore new territory.

In Zen Buddhism, a religion that emphasizes the attainment of enlightenment, this state of mind in which anything seems possible is called *Beginner's Mind*. It is a state in which we put aside what we think we know, along with our limiting points of view and assumptions, and thereby unpredictable results are possible. New opportunities open up, seemingly out of nowhere, and we are able to set a new course of action. Since we are no longer focused on the limitations of old beliefs, or karmic patterns, sometimes the new prospects that become available may seem outside of our scope of thinking. Even if they don't seem familiar, this state of mind is more in tune with your soul wisdom and authentic self.

When I think of Beginner's Mind, I think of the tarot card picturing the Fool. Dressed as a vagabond, standing on a precipice, the Fool is about to step into a fertile void abounding with potentialities. Zero is the number that is attributed to the Fool, for its symbol is nothingness.

In short, when you are in Beginner's Mind, you are free from the shackles of the past. The future beckons with new experiences rather than "the same old same old." Your cup is empty, with plenty of room to be filled with new experiences.

In Rachel's case, which we'll explore in the next section, this state of mind took hold after she cleared her karmic pattern, discovered her spiritual lesson, and risked taking new actions. And it was marked by her life taking a dramatic change for the better.

Free to Be Creative

Rachel came into my office for a healing session because she was suffering from chronic neck pain. Years before, she had been diagnosed with a pinched nerve and was prescribed painkillers to alleviate the problem. However, the pain only worsened, so the doctor prescribed OxyContin. Rachel became addicted to this new medication to the point that she admitted herself into a rehab program. When she was released, she began searching for holistic therapies to bring her healing. She saw my name listed at a healing center and called me for an appointment.

As soon as Rachel went into a state of deep relaxation, my hands were drawn to her neck. The moment I placed my hands on her neck, I felt the anger she had lodged in her throat. An image of a dark-haired man and a name came into my awareness.

"Who's John?" I asked.

"That's my husband's name," she whispered.

"Why are you so mad at him?" I asked.

"He won't let me be me!" she shouted. As I gently held Rachel's neck and channeled Reiki healing energy, Rachel told me how terrible her life had become.

"For twenty-five years, I devoted my life to my husband and children. I always sacrificed my needs for the sake of peace in the family. Not only was I the cook, maid, chauffeur, and personal secretary, I managed the budget and took care of our taxes. I made sure our house and car were maintained and repaired and that the dog got to the vet. Now that the kids are grown up and gone from the house, I want to do things I enjoy. But John won't let me."

Rachel began to cry. "Over the years, John and I have grown further and further apart. The only thing he cares about outside of work is sitting at the computer surfing the Internet.

"He'll never go to a concert or movie with me. I either go out with a girlfriend or go alone. He's rude and puts me down. If I'm playing a CD in the kitchen, he'll turn it off when he enters the room. If I set the watercolor paintings I created on the mantle, he'll take them down. When I told him I was going to get a healing treatment, he said, 'You're crazy—that's nothing but voodoo!'"

I asked Rachel to imagine that her pain was leaving her like a cloud of smoke. She took a deep breath, which helped her to release the frustration from every cell of her being.

Then she sighed. "The pain in my neck is gone," she said.

Rachel already knew the action she needed to take going forward: she needed to speak up for herself rather than be a doormat to her husband.

After a few treatments, Rachel felt stronger and more confident. She then called to tell me the outcome of her previous session. "We're getting divorced! When I told John to stop being mean to me, he packed a suitcase and left. I feel such a sense of relief that I have a voice again. For the first time in years, when I woke up and saw the sun shining through my window, I felt grateful and glad to be alive."

When I spoke with Rachel a year later, she was busy preparing for a show of her paintings, something she'd always dreamed of. Clearing her karmic pattern had helped free her from an unsatisfying marriage. Although she had never planned on getting divorced, it was the next step she had to take for her soul's growth and well-being.

Exercise:
Step Three: Create—
Identifying Your New Actions

Now you are ready for the third part of the Karmic Pattern Formula—to **create,** or to commit to taking a specific action that works for the highest good of all, while helping you upgrade your behavior and unleash your passion.

In step one, **clarify,** you wrote down areas of your life that weren't working as well as you'd like. You pinpointed exact situations in which these problem areas existed, noting when you played the victim and felt powerless. You uncovered your expectations and assumptions in these areas and observed what you need to communicate instead. You noticed where you'd been holding stress in your body or any illnesses that might be related to each pattern. And you learned what associated behaviors you need to let go of.

In step two, **clear**, you reclaimed your power by committing to take full responsibility for these unwanted conditions. You stopped blaming and complaining, let go of any old ways of being, and upgraded your behavior. Choosing a form of exercise or physical treatment, you released the associated tension from your body. If you had an illness, you examined how it has affected your life. And then, ultimately, you discovered the spiritual lesson connected to your karmic pattern.

Now, in step three, **create**, you are ready to commit to taking a specific future action. You have gained the perspective of the Beginner's Mind and have gotten in touch with your authentic self. Here, you can trust that you know what to do. You do have the answers. You know what needs to be said and with whom you need to communicate.

Take a deep breath and go within yourself. Now write down your courses of action. For instance, if you want to sell your artwork, you may want a local gallery to represent you. If so, which gallery? Whom do you need to contact? Do you have your work photographed so you can easily show it to people? Write down all the actions you need to take to achieve your goals. Affirm that your action is for the highest good of all.

When will you accomplish your goal? Set a date and mark it in your appointment calendar. Finally, write down the names of people who will support you in taking these actions and make you accountable.

By completing this process, your life will change in a positive manner. You'll feel more true to yourself, and thereby have more energy to accomplish greater things.

The Karmic Pattern Formula in Action

Now that you know how to use the Karmic Pattern Formula, you can apply it to help you transform all the unwanted conditions on your list. Each time you do, it will be a unique experience for you, bringing about different insights. You can also continue to use the formula to gain power in any challenging situation that seems overwhelming. The important thing is to practice owning your responsibility and to give up blaming, complaining, and assuming. Keep looking for the spiritual lesson in every encounter. By constantly training yourself to actively use the Karmic Pattern Formula, you will find that, after time, using it will become second nature. And as a result, you'll be able to move through the rest of your life with greater ease.

Chapter Four

CHOOSE INTEGRITY

Moral accountability is at the base of human integrity and is the foundation of one's spiritual core. In this chapter, you will learn how to assess your integrity by examining where you have broken your contracts with yourself, with others, and with the environment, and discover ways to restore these areas of your life back to wholeness.

The Importance of Integrity

Keeping promises is a big part of integrity. When you do what you say you will do, life moves with ease. If you show up for work on time and do your job, you have income. If you pay your bills, you have food, shelter, and transportation. When you honor your commitments to your family and friends, you have relationships that matter.

Sometimes it is easier to keep agreements with others rather than with yourself because the consequences of broken promises to others are more obvious. Not paying bills leaves you homeless and hungry. Being unfaithful to your spouse is grounds for a divorce. Getting caught running a red light brings a traffic fine.

It is also important to keep your promises to yourself, because if you don't, you suffer the costs. When you cheat on your diet, you send a message to yourself that you lack self-discipline. If you want a clean car yet never find the time to clear out those piles of trash in the back seat, you're making a silent statement that you are not important, which affects your self-confidence. Placing what you need and want last on your to-do list can lead to feelings of insecurity. If you do not respect yourself, you can't expect others to treat you like you matter.

Being true to your values, beliefs, and standards is essential to having healthy self-esteem, for if you constantly sell out on yourself, you'll feel worthless—you won't trust your choices or have faith in your dreams.

If you don't have a strong internal core built on integrity, you'll lack clarity and be out of touch with what's important to you. If you are unaware of your priorities, you waste time responding to the demands of your circumstances, or fritter away your life on trivial distractions, instead of creating what matters to you most.

Damaged Integrity

If you find yourself making the same New Year's resolutions year after year—to stop smoking or lose weight or regain control of your finances, for example—there has been a breach of integrity in your life. You are repeatedly failing to honor your agreements with yourself.

Likewise, if you commit to giving a friend a ride to work while his car is being repaired and then renege at the last minute, your integrity is damaged with another.

Being accountable for your words and actions is a fundamental part of having integrity. Honoring your commitments, keeping your agreements, and doing what you say you'll do make you reliable. If you are reliable, people trust you and feel they can count on you. In turn, a trustworthy person will create lasting relationships much easier than someone who can't be depended on to keep his or her word. Likewise, a reliable worker who can be trusted to do the job is more apt to be successful.

On the other hand, when you don't do what you say you'll do, you leave matters incomplete, and the tendency is to feel guilt and shame and to lose confidence. Your life becomes filled with drama, chaos, and struggle.

Other behaviors that can sabotage your integrity include holding onto unresolved issues, which drain your energy as you waste time worrying or rehashing past matters over and over in your mind. It's difficult to be in the present moment or plan for the future if you are consumed by the past, so you easily fall into the trap of feeling cynical or resigned.

Leaving different areas of your life incomplete can leak away your precious energy as well. Such incompletion might include something as simple as failing to return an item you borrowed and can range to more serious matters, such as dropping out of college and never earning your degree.

Unfinished projects also clutter your physical space and become roadblocks to creativity. Projects—such as the half-knitted sweater stuffed in the closet or the disassembled antique car in the garage waiting to be restored, and even the expired food in the refrigerator—can all become barriers that inhibit our ability to move forward.

In addition, sometimes we hang onto things that we don't need or can't use. Being surrounded by these objects from the past, which are no longer relevant, keeps us stuck in old emotional "scripts" (automatic childish reactions) and outdated ways of thinking. Holding onto them, we tend to feel exhausted and overwhelmed.

Use the following checklist to help you determine whether you may be practicing behavior that is sabotaging your integrity.

Exercise: Integrity Checklist

Answer the following questions in your journal:

- Do you give your word to people without realistically considering whether you can really deliver on it?

- Do you overcommit yourself?

- Do you have bills or fines that are overdue?

- Are you lax in your health and dental exams?
- Do you have food in your kitchen that's aged beyond the expiration date?
- Do you cheat on your diet?
- Do you have clothes in your closet that don't fit or are out of style?
- Do you have broken agreements with family members?
- Is your office bulletin board full of outdated material?
- Are your projects being worked on according to schedule?
- Are you doing something you don't want to do?
- Can you think of any other area in which your integrity is lacking?

If you answered yes to any of the above questions, use the following exercises to restore your integrity, both with yourself and with others.

Exercise: Restoring Your Integrity

You'll need a new page in your journal and a pen. Take a few deep breaths to center yourself before writing answers to the following questions:

1. What is incomplete for you in these areas?
   - relationships
   - your body
   - family
   - work

- finances
- education
- home
- projects
- the environment

Write down anything that comes to mind that may be incomplete, and take note of any body sensations or emotions you may be feeling as you go through the exercise.

2. Now write down what steps you need to take to complete each incompletion. For example, do you need to communicate? Do you need to forgive someone? If you need to finish a project, when will you have it done? Or do you need to throw things away to declutter your life?

3. Schedule each completion goal in your appointment calendar. Try to tackle as many items as possible to rid yourself of anything that is weighing you down; begin with the small, easy things before taking on tougher burdens.

As you begin to cross items off your lists, new opportunities will open in your life—because when integrity is restored, peace, clarity, and ease can prevail.

Unspoken Contracts

Oftentimes we have unspoken agreements with others that need to be changed. For instance, in a relationship you may be the one who loads the dishwasher every day, even though you never volunteered to have that job. Or you may be the one who automatically pays the dinner bill when you dine out with your family. Another example: you wind up being the designated driver whenever you go out with friends.

Sometimes, however, these contracts aren't fair and need to be renegotiated. Take, for instance, the unspoken contract that Ellen, a client, had. Ellen came in for a reading because she was upset with her boyfriend, Michael. Ellen was always available when Michael phoned her. She'd always get back to him, even if it was just with a text message to set a time to talk later, for instance, when she was busy working. But often when Ellen called him, even after she'd leave several messages saying that it was important to connect, he wouldn't even return her call.

During her reading, Ellen concluded that their mutual contract with each other was out of balance. Ellen had communicated that she wanted more from him, time after time, but he was unable to give it. Michael wasn't giving her what she needed, so she broke up with him. Their contract was terminated.

Another thing to note about contracts is that they often need to be renegotiated over the years because over time, integrity lapses and relationships change. Take the unspoken contracts of family members for example. Parents and children generally know what to expect from one another. However, a parent with a two-year-old child has different responsibilities than a parent with a thirty-year-old, so hopefully their contracts change as the relationship develops through the years.

Siblings also formulate unspoken contracts with each other in childhood that need to change. In their youth, the oldest child might be responsible for the younger brother or sister. One sibling may take on a caretaker role as their parents grow old. Or, even as an adult, the baby of the family may resist growing up in order to be loyal to an old relational contract with older siblings or parents.

Exercise: Rebalancing Unspoken Contracts with Others

Take a moment to go within and center yourself. Then consider whether your unspoken contracts with the following people are out of balance:

- your parents, siblings, or other family members
- your children
- your spouse or significant other
- your friends or neighbors
- your employer, employees, or coworkers
- any other relationships

Now ask yourself the following: What new conversations need to take place to renegotiate your unspoken contracts? What do you need to say? When are you committed to having these talks?

An Unspoken Contract with Earth

Sitting on the floor of a small ceremonial room, with chickens squawking in the background and motor taxis roaring down the dirt road, I asked Paolo—a Shipibo shaman in Pucallpa, Peru—his opinion on the recent disastrous earthquakes, tsunamis, hurricanes, and other foreboding earth changes. My sweaty palm held the digital recorder propped on my knee, and beads of perspiration pooled at my temples from the heat and humidity.

Paolo lowered his gaze and said in somber tone, "The earth has ended her contract with us."

"Please explain," I answered with wide-eyed curiosity.

"Our agreement is that people live in harmony with nature. We haven't kept our promise, but instead have ravaged and polluted the environment, so the nature spirits are reneging on their contract to protect us."

If there is anyone who knows how to communicate with earth spirits, it's the Amazonian shamans. Over thousands of years, their ancestors have learned the medicinal properties of the plants by observation trial and error. Paolo's grandparents thought of the rainforest as a pharmacy, supplying people with remedies for every ailment. They learned what plants cured specific diseases as well as the appropriate dosages to use. They would never do anything to harm their environment, for they knew that in so doing they'd only be hurting themselves.

One goes through vigorous training to become a shaman and undergoes a purification process that involves a strict diet and abstaining from sex and alcohol. Self-discipline is at the core of this process because the occupation holds such great responsibility that one needs to have impeccable integrity to fulfill it. In addition, practicing shamanic healing entails communicating with plants, which are pure, and such communication requires one to be sensitive and spiritually developed. Shamans believe that every plant has a healing song called an *icaro*. Sometimes these songs have actual Shipibo words, but other times they're in another language or have no words.

In turn, every shaman has different icaros, depending on how many plant diets he has had. At the initial stage of learning, the shaman goes on a plant diet. He is allowed to eat one meal a day at lunchtime. For his other meals, he drinks a strong tea or infusion made from that plant, purifying his body so that he can connect with the plant's spirit. After a while, the plant's energy begins to merge with the shaman. He becomes so in tune with the plant that he may hear an icaro in a dream, almost as if he were downloading the song from the plant.

The day I arrived in Pucallpa, I had the opportunity to experience the healing power of icaros. I had a splitting headache. It felt like there was an axe embedded in my skull. Miguel, another shaman who was teaching at the school of traditional medicine, invited me to rest on a cushion in the ceremonial room. As he massaged my abdomen, my body relaxed. He then gently touched my head and appeared to be listening for something. I imagined that he was making some diagnosis just by feeling my energy. Miguel silently asked the plants for help, and a moment later he sang an icaro. His voice was beautiful, soothing, and yet charged with power. The vibration of the plant's song acted like a needle positioned on an acupuncture point. I felt a rush of energy go through my body, and tears welled up in my eyes. As I cried, I felt enormous relief. A moment later, my headache was gone.

Miguel went on to sing another song, and my sadness was replaced with a sense of peace and well-being. The healing took about fifteen minutes and was as sophisticated as any other established vibrational healing modality I had experienced.

When I asked Miguel how we could restore our integrity with Mother Nature, he said that it was complicated and would take time. He said that we couldn't just keep exploiting our resources because such behavior was creating havoc, and that many political changes had to be made, including new laws and regulations. He also felt, however, that if individuals shifted their awareness and became more respectful to nature, we would begin to heal our broken contract and restore balance.

Since climate change is more and more in the news, people are beginning to go green and live more sustainably. But we still have a long way to go. Many may still be unaware of the damage we do to the earth, because our thoughtless behavior is ingrained in our culture. It is part of our ignorance, avidya. The fast-food industry has conditioned us to mindlessly throw away Styrofoam cups and plastic food containers. Advertisers have brainwashed us to believe that poisoning the ground with pesticides doesn't hurt anything. And gas companies have convinced people to allow them to frack their land even though it endangers the water supply.

One summer, my husband and I rented a house in a quiet neighborhood at the eastern shore. The house was nestled among loblolly pine trees, where flickers, blue jays, and egrets perched throughout the day. One morning, our peace was disturbed by the sound of chainsaws buzzing. We were horrified to discover a crew of men cutting down a grove of healthy trees in the neighbor's backyard. Three deer entered our yard, looking bewildered and stressed by the thunderous sound of forty-foot trees toppling to the ground. Cardinals were frantically calling out to one another as their homes were being destroyed.

My husband, angered not only by the obnoxiously loud noise but also by the brutality of the action, went to ask the foreman of the tree-service crew why they were butchering perfectly good trees. The trees weren't a threat to the house, they had no diseases, and the owner wasn't clearing the land to build on.

The foreman replied, "The owners don't want them trees no more."

This shortsighted mentality toward the environment is also present in the city. Many communities would rather cut down their streets' trees than rake up the leaves in the fall.

However, when people make choices based on personal convenience rather than on sustainability, everyone's survival is threatened. When trees shade houses and buildings, they release moisture into the air, minimizing the need for air-conditioning and reducing the greenhouse effect. Trees also shade parking lots that hold heat from the sun, bringing temporary relief from oven-degree temperatures. In addition, trees and plants absorb major sounds from freeways and airports, thereby controlling noise pollution. When planted on hillsides, trees prevent soil erosion and destructive mudslides.

Finally, the tree canopy provides an ecosystem for birds, small animals, and insects—and these creatures have a right to survive just as humans do. They work together in complex ways to maintain clean air and soil. For true sustainability, we must protect the habitats of these creatures and be responsible for managing our resources. We need to be true to ourselves, but we must also, as the Native Americans would say, respect "all our relations."

Exercise:
Rebalancing Your Contract with Earth

The following exercise is designed to help you examine your integrity in regard to your connection to the earth. To begin, write down any insights you have about your relationship to your environment as you answer the following questions:

- Do you know where your household trash ends up after it is taken from your curbside?

- How many pounds of garbage does your household throw out each week?

- How can you create less waste?

- Do you recycle?
- As a consumer, do you buy environment-friendly products?
- Do you properly dispose of toxic waste?
- When you purchase a product, do you consider where the product will wind up after you've used it?
- Do you compost?
- How many plants in your backyard can you name?
- How many trees on your property or in your neighborhood do you know by name?
- What environmental crisis is your city dealing with?
- What can you do to upgrade your relationship to the earth? What actions do you need to take? When are you going to start?

Another simple thing that all of us can do to be more in touch with nature, and thus work toward restoring our contract with earth, is to say a prayer at mealtime. Because grocery stores are so abundant, it's easy to take our sustenance for granted. But when you take time to make the connection between food and life, realizing you'd die without it, you see how precious it is. The practice of saying thank you to Mother Earth before eating changes your state of mind to gratitude, which brings peace and inner calm.

Maintaining Integrity (Yamas)

Now that you have restored your integrity, you can use wisdom from yoga to help you maintain it. Yoga, the ancient science that acknowledges the connection between body and mind, has become very popular in recent years. Many think yoga is just a form of exercise; however, it's also a philosophy that gives guidelines to live a happy, meaningful life.

When I took a yoga teacher training class years ago, I learned that yoga postures, or *asanas,* were developed to tone and cleanse the body, and the *yamas,* translated to mean discipline or restraint, were designed to purify the mind.

Yamas are basically principles that can help you build an ethical foundation for spiritual development. As you change and upgrade your behaviors, yamas can help you integrate more compassion and awareness into your life so that you become more conscious and thereby maintain your integrity. The five yamas described in the ancient text of the *Yoga Sutras* are also known as the great universal vows. They are as follows:

1. Nonviolence. *Ahimsa*: Cause no harm to yourself or others. Be kind and thoughtful, and show consideration to people and things.

2. Truthfulness. *Satya*: Practice honesty with yourself and others.

3. Don't steal. *Asteya*: Never take what belongs to another without permission, and never use something borrowed for a different purpose than intended or beyond the time agreed upon by its owner.

4. Moderation. *Brahmacharya*: Be responsible for your sexuality and intimacy needs.

5. Avoid greed. *Aparigraha:* Simplify your life and take only what is necessary.

Yamas are not about moralizing what is right and wrong, as are other types of religious doctrines. The purpose of living according to these principles is to develop a strong character, enabling you to connect with your soul, and thereby, to feel happy and fulfilled.

Journaling Exercise: Yamas in Your Life

Find a comfortable place to write where you won't be disturbed. You may choose a quiet spot in nature, in your home surrounded by relaxing music, or even in a noisy café. Whatever you prefer, give yourself at least a half an hour to complete the exercise.

1. Nonviolence in Your Life (Ahimsa)

At the root, ahimsa means maintaining compassion toward yourself and others. It also means being kind and treating all things with care. Ahimsa is the umbrella under which the other yamas fall. Some interpret ahimsa in their lives by becoming vegans or by avoiding wearing leather and fur. Others refuse to kill insects that wander into the house, putting them outside instead. And yet others understand the term to mean not watching violent television shows or movies. What does it represent to you?

Complete the following exercises in your journal to help you determine how you can practice ahimsa in your life:

- List at least ten actions you can take to be more loving to yourself.

- Write another list of how you can show more care to your environment.

- On another page, list how you can be more compassionate to others. Note whether particular people come to mind. Write down everything that comes into your awareness.

- Are you aware of when you are causing harm to others?

2. Truthfulness in Your Life (Satya)

Satya means truth, in particular, speaking honestly without harming others. Gossiping, cursing, lying, and being verbally abusive are ways we spiritually misuse speech. Before talking, consider what you are saying and how your communication may affect others.

How can you practice satya in your life? To answer this question, use your journal to do the following:

- Write down situations in which you find it difficult to communicate. Are there certain people that you have difficulty being open and honest with? Where do you catch yourself being inauthentic? Now using the information you come up with about yourself through journaling, try taking on one area of communication in the next month that you can transform.

- Keeping silent can be the most powerful form of communication. Look at areas where you talk too much. Can you keep a secret?

- Work on giving up one of the four negative speech patterns (gossiping, cursing, lying, and being verbally abusive) for twenty-one days. Write down your commitment in your journal. For example, try giving up cursing. Each day, track your progress. Once you've mastered eliminating one negative way of speaking, pick another way.

3. Do Not Steal in Your Life (Asteya)

Asteya means not stealing someone else's possessions, spouse, or job. It also means not taking that which isn't offered—including someone's time, energy, or ideas.

One reason you might want to steal is the belief that there isn't enough for everyone. Another motive may be the idea that you do not have the power to get what you want. So the antidote to this spiritual malady would be to release the underlying false belief in scarcity and to instead affirm the idea of abundance.

In your journal, discover how you can practice asteya by answering the following questions:

- Do you borrow things from others and forget to return them?

- Do you waste other people's time by being late?

- Do you have affairs with married men or women?

- Do you make personal calls while at work?

4. Moderation in Your Life (Brahmacharya)

Brahmacharya means turning your attention toward the divine and, therefore, away from sensual indulgence. When the mind is not continually distracted by thoughts of food, sex, and other such diversions, you can become more aware of your inner fulfillment.

Practicing brahmacharya means consciously choosing to express your soul's purpose, rather than to frivolously dissipate your energy pursuing fleeting pleasures. For example, sexual activity is not bad. However, your life force is limited, and sexual promiscuity depletes it. As such, the practice of brahmacharya is not some puritanical form of moralizing you, but rather a reminder to use your energy wisely.

How can you practice brahmacharya? Answer the following questions in your journal:

- Do you use your sexuality for power and control?
- When do you catch yourself overeating, overspending, or drinking too much?
- Do you have too much spare time and thereby become preoccupied with food or sex?
- Do you misuse your sexual energy by flirting with people who are in committed relationships?

5. Avoid Greed in Your Life (Aparigraha)

Aparigraha means nonpossessiveness or abstaining from material greed. Focusing on gathering material objects can create stress because items can be lost, broken, or stolen, so it is best not to acquire more than you minimally need. Things take energy to be maintained and, even when discarded, use up valuable resources, as many objects are still unable to decompose in the landfills.

Oftentimes, however, our material possessions run our lives. Many people are enslaved by jobs they hate just to pay off their debt, which they incurred in order to buy and keep things they don't use.

When we become nonpossessive, or unattached to things, we become impartial to material objects and free up energy, allowing ourselves to more easily express unconditional love and affection toward the nonmaterial.

How can you practice aparigraha? Use your journal to address the following points:

- Do you appreciate what you have?
- How much is enough? Can you be happy with less?
- Cultivating an "attitude of gratitude" opens the door to receiving abundance. In what ways can you take on such an attitude on a day-to-day basis?
- Designate some time to clear out cluttered closets, drawers, attics, or basements. Practice generosity by giving away what you no longer use or need.

Restored Wholeness

By this point in the book, you've discovered the importance of integrity and how to restore it. You've cleaned up your broken agreements, renewed your contracts with others, and gained a new perspective on your relationship with the earth. By finishing what was left incomplete, you have also sealed any energy drains that existed within you and reclaimed your power. Finally, you have discovered the wisdom of ancient yoga, which has provided you with a code of ethics that you can practice to strengthen your character. To continue on your way toward strength, in the next chapter you'll gain clarity about what you really want in life and your purpose for being here.

Chapter Five

CHOOSE PURPOSE

Everyone wants happiness, but few people understand that external things—having the right house, a trendy car, a prestigious job, and fashionable friends—only bring temporary fulfillment. Things, people, and jobs come and go. However, when you discover your true purpose for your life, you can find lasting inner peace. In this chapter, you'll connect with your soul's intention for being here. You'll learn how to align your everyday choices with the divine plan of your life and use natural plant-based remedies to support your continued growth.

Your Heart's Desire

Heart disease, the number-one killer in America, may be linked to deeper issues than obesity and high cholesterol levels. Since mind, body, and spirit are holistically interconnected, emotional and mental states have a cumulative impact on health and well-being. If you are conflicted because you are doing something that, deep down, you don't want to do, it is bound to cause stress.

If you live a stressful lifestyle, your immune system is weakened. Your body reacts by getting sick or showing some symptom of pain. When in pain, it's natural to want to medicate it by using drugs or alcohol, which often makes matters worse.

If you're stressed out and off center, you are likely to be out of touch with your heart's desire. This leads to making choices that aren't in your best interest. For example, it's easy to get trapped in unsuitable jobs, slaving away the hours to buy things you don't really need. Going into debt is a high price to pay for happiness. Or you may be out of touch with what is really important to you, so you pick the wrong people for partners.

Enthusiasm for life turns into cynicism and resignation if you robotically go through a dull routine of just eating, working, and sleeping. It is easy to become depressed or create a crisis. Take Michel's case, for instance.

Michel's Story

When Michel was a young man, he loved to paint and discovered he had artistic talent. He spent hours watching the way light reflected off a bowl of fruit and was able to see how an orange contained shades of blue in its shadow while its highlights appeared yellow. Michel loved squeezing rich, creamy oil paint out of a tube and spreading it on canvas as if icing a cake, piling the paint into thick mounds like colored custard. But other times, he glazed over the surface with a slick, translucent wash.

Each blank canvas gave him an opportunity to have an adventure. Michel never painted the same picture twice, always finishing a painting in one sitting. Some paintings turned out beautifully, while others failed miserably and wound up in the trash. But the end product wasn't as important as the process of expressing himself.

When Michel painted, he escaped into another world as he focused on his subject, which could be a landscape, person, or still life. A mysterious chemistry happened as a three-dimensional illusion of a vase of flowers emerged from the blank, two-dimensional surface of his canvas. The pink petals of the tulips appeared soft and velvety in contrast to the shiny white porcelain vase. The golden glow of light pouring into the room promised the return of spring. Like magic, Michel captured a moment in time.

But unlike in a snapshot or photograph, the flowers in his painting seemed infused with vigor. They pulsated with vitality. Each brushstroke shimmered with luminosity. It was as though the flowers on his canvas were alive.

However, Michel's parents didn't want their son to grow up to be an artist. They insisted that he learn a practical, well-paying craft and convinced him to major in chemistry. So instead of painting, Michel spent his college years preparing to be a lab technician.

After Michel graduated, he met the woman who would change his destiny—an American art student who was studying in Paris. They married and moved to the United States, where Michel turned the spare bedroom of their apartment into an art studio by setting up his easel and paints. The room had high ceilings and large windows that let in the northern light that was perfect for painting a still life. But, needing money, Michel also took on a full-time job as a house painter.

As time passed, even though oil painting was Michel's passion, he never seemed to have enough time to do it. He spent his weekdays on ladders, rolling paint on walls, while he squeezed in studio time on the weekends.

Ultimately, Michel's lifestyle became so unsatisfying that he dreaded getting out of bed in the morning. He felt trapped and fell into a depression. He hated painting houses and couldn't imagine enduring the drudgery another year. He felt miserable, for he knew he was wasting his talent. His discontent also affected his marriage, and he was getting a divorce.

However, the breakup of Michel's marriage spurred him to look deeply at his priorities. He grappled about what mattered most to him, which was to be an artist.

If I don't fully pursue my dream to be a professional artist, will I live a life of regret? he pondered.

Michel had no idea how he'd ever afford to enroll in art school. But he knew he couldn't live with himself if he never tried to attain his dream.

Michel also knew that he'd have to live frugally if he were to become an artist; there was no way he could afford to have a car or cable television. But he took a leap of faith and applied to a prestigious art college. Not only was he accepted, he was awarded a full scholarship and grant money to support himself through school.

What Michel thought would be a sacrifice wasn't hard at all. He didn't really need a car or cable TV. Because he lived in the city, he found it easy to get around on his bicycle or on public transportation. He discovered he could entertain himself by reading, playing sports, or jogging through the park.

Two years after graduating from art school, Michel had a new life in which he painted canvases every day, instead of houses. Since his schedule wasn't overbooked with distractions, his stress level was low and his creative output was high. Because his paintings were so original and spirited, they were sold in six galleries across the country. He had the time to travel the world to places that inspired him. The legs of his portable oak easel are stained with salt water from the Mediterranean Sea, orange-colored dust from the desert in Arizona, and yellow-ochre clay from the hills of Tuscany.

Michel may not make a million dollars, but his life is rich and purposeful. By setting his priorities and having the courage to pursue his dream, Michel created a great life, filled with work that brings him joy, inspiration, and satisfaction. He lives a life he loves.

Living Life with Purpose

You don't need a crisis to change your life. All you need is to know yourself. Being in touch with your authentic self and what you truly value makes life meaningful.

Following your heart may be easier said than done, for one's mission can often look impossible. It takes courage to have faith in yourself and go after what you want.

You may be tested and have to overcome some obstacle to achieve it. That is where growth occurs. You have to get out of your comfort zone. However, your soul—your spiritual essence that embodies love and is eternal and divine—is on an evolutionary journey and is constantly seeking expansion and growth. Your soul wants new experiences because staying stuck in old patterns hinders development. Your authentic self attracts the right circumstances that provide the opportunity for learning and gaining wisdom.

Sometimes it may appear you don't have a choice as to how you live your life. Perhaps you believe you need to do what your parents want you to do. Or you may know what you want but lack the confidence needed to pursue it. Maybe you don't have enough emotional or financial support to follow your dreams. However, if you get too off track from your true purpose, oftentimes a crisis occurs to force you to confront what matters most. But you don't need a calamity to be your wake-up call; you have the power to change your life at any given moment.

Exercise:
Checking In with Your Purpose

It is easy to fall into habits and routines that are predictable. One way to help see outside of your situation is to do something out of the ordinary. So for this exercise, if you usually stay at home, go to a café you have never patronized—or vice versa. Or try sitting in the park or some other place you normally wouldn't visit. Once you're at this new location, answer the following questions in your journal:

- If your life keeps going the way it's going, how will it turn out thirty years from now?

- Will you be fulfilled in love? Work? Family?

- Will you have regrets?

- Will you have made use of your talents and special gifts?

- What will be the condition of your body? The state of your health?

- Will you have traveled and seen the world?

- Will you have used your resources wisely?

- Will you still be doing things you loved doing when you were a child?

Imagine yourself as ninety years old, lying on your deathbed, reviewing your life. View it like you were watching a movie of yourself. What would you say about your life? Write down your insights. What needs to change? If you had to write a mission statement for your life, what would it be?

Checking In with Your Purpose Meditation

For this meditation, you'll need a deck of Rider-Waite tarot cards. If you don't have one, search for a picture of the Sun tarot card online. This card has an image of a child riding a white pony in bright sunlight. The child's arms are wide open, ready to embrace life. Sunflowers bloom in the background.

In astrology, which is a component part of tarot, the sun rules the heart, the spine, and the ego of an individual. The Sun card signifies your potential to fully express yourself. It represents the main direction of your life and your determination to accomplish what you set out to do. The Sun represents your ability to have the courage to stand up for your beliefs and thereby command respect and authority.

This meditation can help you connect to your inner sun, the center of your being, which holds the key to your purpose. Have your journal and a pen available to write your experience down when you finish.

Place the Sun card before you. Focus on it until you can recall it in your mind's eye. Once you have a sense of what this card looks like, proceed with the following meditation. You may want to record it so that you can be fully in the process.

Begin recording the following script:

Go into a state of relaxation by taking a few deep, connected breaths.

Imagine the Sun card in your mind's eye growing larger and larger until the figures in it become life-size. Step into the card.

The landscape extends out in all directions. As you look around at your environment, you feel the warmth of the sun filling you with strength and vitality. Do you hear any sounds? Do you notice any smells?

You see a white pony standing in front of a wall. Behind it, a row of blooming sunflowers are standing tall. A child runs over to you, smiling and giggling with delight. Take note if the child is male or female.

The child grabs your hand and offers you sunflower seeds, saying, "Here, eat these."

You place them in your mouth. How do they taste?

Immediately, you feel yourself getting lighter and lighter. You begin to regress back in time, back to when you were an innocent child. You feel a sense of overwhelming joy with each breath you take.

All of your cares and concerns melt away and are replaced with feelings of excitement and enthusiasm.

You open your arms wide and twirl around. It feels good to move your body. You feel happy and carefree. Take time to explore and play.

You look up at the sun, but it is so bright, you have to close your eyes. You can feel the warmth of the sun in your heart; when you focus your attention there, you see that your heart is glowing with light. It has an intelligence of its own.

Take a moment to ask it, "What is my purpose?"

Let the response flow into your awareness. The answer may come as a picture, symbol, words, or feelings. Trust what comes.

You open your eyes as you feel the child tugging on your arm while saying, "Come and ride the pony."

You hop on the pony, and it begins to walk down a path. You intuitively know that it is taking you to an important scene. You feel you are riding into the future, a year from now. You are being shown something positive—something for your highest good that will occur in your future a year from now. Let yourself go into the future. This is a message about your purpose. Trust what you see, hear, and feel.

Now the pony is taking you back in time, back to the present. You are feeling light and free … open to life … empowered. You are aligned with your purpose.

You return to the wall with the sunflower garden and hop off the pony. When your feet touch the ground you are back into your present body at your current age.

You wave good-bye to the child and call out, "Thank you."

You take one last look around. You step out of the card. When you do, it shrinks back into its normal size.

End your recording.

Write down your experience in your journal. What did the environment look like? Did you hear sounds or notice smells? Was the child male or female? Did you recognize him or her as someone you know? What did the ride into the future look like? What were you shown? How did it feel? What was the message from your heart?

Write a positive statement, affirming that you can attain the purpose you were shown.

Your Purpose in the World (Dharma)

You are here to make a contribution to the world. Great or small, everyone has a purpose. In Eastern philosophy, this purpose is called *dharma*. Metaphysical teacher, best-selling author, and past-life expert Dick Sutphen describes dharma in his book *Predestined Love* as "your duty to yourself and society." Some view dharma as your mission in life. By following your mission or purpose, you evolve and grow with ease as you fulfill your commitment to serve humanity. You gain spiritual wisdom while at the same time gaining worldly happiness.

However, everyone has a different purpose. One person's dharma may be to marry and raise a family. Another person's may be to become an environmental activist. Yet another may need to be a schoolteacher, educating and enlightening the youth. Steve Jobs's dharma brought new technology that enhanced the lives of millions, while Julia Child brought gourmet French cooking to the average household. Others, such as Gandhi and Martin Luther King, transformed whole cultures.

Famous or not, most people don't discover their purpose by meditating in an isolated cave. It is while we are engaged in the world that we learn our spiritual lessons and serve our purpose. For you exist not only as a separate identity, with a body and personality, you also exist in the hearts and minds of others. Your participation counts. If you've ever gone to a memorial service for someone who has died, this is obvious; who you are to others lives on. This does not only apply after you die, but also in the present. You have a say in how you occur for others through how you behave and communicate.

Living Purposefully (Niyamas)

In American society, our success is determined by what we do and own. But the yogis believe that how you are being and acting is more important. In the last chapter, you learned that incorporating the yamas in your life purifies your consciousness so that you are more in touch with your spiritual nature. Practicing the yamas helps you develop positive attitudes and behaviors relating to people and things outside of yourself.

Niyamas, another aspect of yoga, translates to mean "observance." While the yamas are universal, the niyamas are personal. These practices extend the ethical codes of conduct provided in the yamas. Niyamas are rules of self-discipline to follow to help you relate to yourself. Practicing the niyamas can help you to be free from attachments that cause suffering. The five major niyamas are as follows:

1. Purity. *Saucha:* Practice cleanliness.

2. Contentment. *Santosh:* Be happy with what you have.

3. Austerity. *Tapas:* Apply self-discipline.

4. Self-Study. *Swadhyaya:* Know your authentic self.

5. Surrender to the Divine. *Ishvar Pranidhana:* Develop a relationship with the Higher Power.

These principles can help you cultivate actions and attitudes that connect you to your authentic self. Practicing the niyamas helps you maintain a positive state of being and gives you the self-discipline and inner strength necessary to progress along your path of purpose.

The niyamas can help you cultivate and develop moral virtues that are in alignment with your spirit. When you are aligned with your spirit, you are able to make life-affirming choices. Ultimately, when positive choices are followed by constructive actions, the law of karma brings positive consequences.

Journaling Exercise: Niyamas in Your Life

1. Purity in Your Life (Saucha)

Saucha means purity of body, heart, and mind. In yoga, the body is viewed as a vehicle for the soul's expression. When your body is free from disease, you have more time and energy to devote to your spiritual growth and to fulfilling your dharma. Here are some simple steps that can help you maintain good health:

- Eat foods that are free from preservatives and pesticides.
- Choose to eat fruits and vegetables.
- Live in a toxic-free environment.
- Exercise on a routine basis.
- Practice personal hygiene.
- Get enough rest and sleep.

Some yogis like to fast occasionally as a way to cleanse the body of impurities. Others like to take saunas or steam baths. And others find taking spa treatments, such as wraps or mud baths, to be a therapeutic way to detoxify the body.

But it is also important to live in a clean environment. Keeping your house neat creates a more peaceful atmosphere, making it easier for you to thrive. The Chinese art of *feng shui* also supports this view, for vital energy becomes blocked or stagnant in a cluttered environment, as it cannot flow freely.

If your living space is messy, it may affect your ability to think clearly. Since a chaotic space doesn't support calmness, you might become restless and fall into worrying. It may become difficult to focus, leading to feeling anxious.

Keeping your mind pure from negative thoughts comes under the practice of saucha. If you watch violent television programs, you plant seeds of violence in your consciousness. Watching films or reading novels with graphic tales of perversity also negatively affects peace and serenity.

Saucha also promotes having a pure heart, which means not carrying anger, resentment, and hostility. Focusing on gratitude and forgiveness is the key to finding emotional peace.

In your journal, answer the following questions to discover how you can cultivate saucha:

- Are you taking care of your body by providing healthy food, exercise, detoxifying treatments, and rest? If not, what steps can you take to expand your ability to take care of your body?

- Does your living space nurture you? If it doesn't, how can you make it better?

- Are you taking care of your mental well-being by watching television programs or movies that inspire you and uplift your spirit? What kind of messages are you taking in from watching television, surfing the Internet, or reading? Are they life affirming, or do they promote fear, powerlessness, and worry? How can you improve the way you nurture your mental well-being?

- Are you taking care of your emotional health? Is there someone you need to forgive? Do you need to make peace with someone? Are you spending enough time doing things you enjoy?

2. Contentment in Your Life (Santosh)

Santosh means accepting your life exactly the way it is—and exactly the way it isn't. It is easy to fret about the past and worry about the future, which leads to missing being in the present. It takes practice to create contentment. You don't have to wait for circumstances to look a certain way to be happy. You can generate happiness on your own.

Sometimes I catch myself feeling stressed out while I'm driving around town running errands. It could be a beautiful day with the sun shining. All of my bills are paid. None of my friends or family are in the hospital. In reality, nothing is wrong. Yet I need to check in to remind myself that I can opt to shift my state of mind. Instead of reacting to traffic with annoyance, I can choose to be patient.

I once noticed that if a certain friend who had a lot of problems called, my automatic response was to ask, "What's wrong?" She would then unload all of her crisis and upset onto me. I fell into a trap of supporting her being a drama queen. One day I got fed up and decided to change my role.

When I started applying a "nothing is wrong" attitude when she called, my friend stopped dumping her drama on me and we had conversations that were more enlivening.

Another way to shift discontent is not to dwell on what you lack and to have gratitude for what you have. Instead of getting grumpy when it rains on your vacation, find a positive alternative. Perhaps you can be grateful for a day to lounge around, or to snuggle up with a good book, or to write a letter to an old friend. Sometimes breaking out of a routine way of thinking can open a new door of creativity.

How can you practice santosh in your life? To answer this question, use your journal to do the following exercise:

- Create a gratitude journal by each day writing three things you are grateful for.

- Check in with yourself on the hour to become more aware of your emotional state. If you are feeling anxious and stressed, see if you are willing to shift. If you are, take a few deep breaths. Focus on one of these affirmations, or make one up.
  - My life is in divine order.
  - Everything is happening as it should.
  - I have enough time, energy, wisdom, and money to accomplish what I need to do.
  - Nothing is wrong.

- If you are feeling anxious, check to see if your integrity is intact. Do you need to clean up a broken agreement with yourself or another? Are you procrastinating instead of taking a necessary action?

- Stop relating to people as though there is a problem, even if there is something wrong. People are bigger than their problems. Relate to their bigness, not their smallness.

3. Austerity in Your Life (Tapas)

Tapas means self-discipline; however, it does not mean austerity to the point that causes suffering. Applying a fiery discipline is necessary to continually burn the blocks to spiritual growth. You need to make a constant effort to keep fit in all areas of your life. If you are committed to something, your actions must be aligned to that commitment. You can't allow procrastination, laziness, or other negative behaviors to impede you.

If you want to have a healthy body, it is important to exercise on a regular basis. You can't just go to the gym or yoga studio once and say, "That's it. I exercised. I'm fit forever." You keep toned by incorporating exercise into your daily routine. Applying tapas means getting yourself to your fitness class whether you feel like it or not. You exercise or practice yoga because you are committed to health. It's easy to find an excuse for not doing it, such as "I don't feel great today," or allow a circumstance to interfere with your commitment, such as choosing to chat on the phone instead of getting to your class on time. A teacher of mine once said, "You either have the results you want to have in your life or the reasons why you don't." Applying tapas burns off the excuses, and you keep your commitment. You build muscle in the area of honoring what is most important to you.

You can apply the principle of tapas to other areas of your life. If you want a happy marriage, you have to make the effort to maintain a dynamic partnership. You can't expect to say, "I compromised what I wanted to do one time and let my mate have his way," and expect you will never need to again. You have to continuously practice being reliable, trustworthy, and supportive, and exhibit other positive qualities in order to preserve a good relationship. Sometimes it means sticking through the hard times when the going gets rough.

Whether you want to be a great artist, a millionaire, or a good parent, you have to apply consistency in striving toward your goals. Successful people honor their commitments. Routinely, whether they are in the mood or not, they practice their craft and polish their skills. When they are tested, they don't bail out. They confront their challenges and work through difficulties.

How can you practice tapas in your life? To answer this question, use your journal to do the following exercise:

- List areas of your life where you need to apply self-discipline.

- Pick one area to start with. Set a goal around this area. For instance, the goal could be to practice yoga twice a week.

- Next, add the goal to your appointment calendar. For example, if your goal is to practice yoga, write down the time and location of the class. It is in your schedule, and nothing interferes with it. Pretend it is written in stone.

If a friend calls and asks you to go out during this time, your answer is, "I'm not available at that time."

- Keep your commitment. Go to your class, no matter what. Be there, even if you don't feel like it. Attend, even though you'd rather watch television.

- Once you've mastered this goal, move on to another area that needs tapas and repeat the steps.

4. Self-Study in Your Life (Swadhyaya)

Swadhyaya means self-study. When you know yourself, you are able to make better choices. If you know you have an artistic temperament, then you can conclude that you probably won't be happy with a career as a lab technician. If you hate cold weather, you can deduce that living in Alaska may not be conducive to your well-being. Alternately, if you are gay but not in touch with yourself, then you could find yourself living unfulfilled in a heterosexual relationship.

A great way of getting to know yourself is through astrology. Horoscopes, which mean "map of the hour," can help you gain a better understanding of your true nature and temperament. The birth chart pinpoints strengths and weaknesses, karmic patterns from other lifetimes that are ingrained and comfortable, as well as what you are here to learn. Just knowing your Sun sign is a start to beginning to know yourself.

You may want to take up a practice of self-study, such as knowing your horoscope, learning your numerology, having your palm or tarot cards read, or having your handwriting analyzed.

If you know yourself, you can relate to others in a healthier way. You won't rely on someone else to make you happy; you'll understand what you need and be able to provide your own fulfillment. Chances are you will avoid getting trapped in codependent entanglements.

Knowing yourself is an ongoing process. Life provides you with endless opportunities to learn and grow. Every circumstance that you attract into your life can help you discover something about yourself. When viewed in this context, life is an exciting adventure.

How can you practice swadhyaya? Answer the following questions in your journal:

- What have you learned from your successes? Failures?

- What are your ten best qualities? How could you express more of them in your everyday life?

- What are your ten worst qualities? Picking one from your list, how could you transform it into a positive trait?

5. Surrender to the Divine in Your Life (Ishvara Pranidhana)

Ishvara pranidhana translates to mean "surrendering to the Higher Power." This Higher Power—whether you call it God, Goddess, or Infinite Intelligence—is all loving, knowing, and caring. It does not promote suffering or harm to anyone or anything.

This niyama is much like two steps of the philosophy of the twelve-step program: One is to acknowledge that there is a greater power that can restore sanity. Two is to decide to turn one's will and one's life over to this Higher Power.

Sometimes it is easy to be so focused on the end result that one doesn't enjoy the process of getting there. But this niyama reminds us of the saying "It is not a matter of whether you win or lose; it's how you play the game that counts." There is much in your life you can't control, so you can't be attached to outcomes. Practicing ishvara pranidhana involves learning to be more fully alive in each moment, without thinking about the future or the past. When you give up your attachment to an outcome, the quality of your actions will improve.

Incorporating ishvara pranidhana in your life will help you develop faith in yourself, for the yogis believe that a spark of the divine lives within you, everyone, and everything. You don't have to look outside yourself, for all the answers you seek are within you.

Sometimes we are forced to surrender when circumstances bring death, loss, illness, or other types of crisis. Bad things happen to good people. Having faith that everything happens for a reason can bring peace. Sometimes challenges can help us develop strength or connect to inner resources we didn't know we had.

How can you practice ishvara pranidhana? Here are a couple ways to help you learn to surrender to the eternal and divine:

- *Om* is the sound symbol of ishvara. Practicing chanting om, either out loud or silently in your mind, can help you connect to this omnipresent source that permeates everyone and everything. Sit quietly with your eyes closed for a few minutes each day while focusing on the sound of om.

- Go to your favorite beach. Wade out into the water. When you feel ready, consciously make an effort to float or dive into the next wave. Let go—surrender. Allow the surf to gently carry you back to the shore.

Everything Has a Purpose

If you live within the context that your life has meaning and purpose, it will give you power. For instance, years ago, someone whom I trusted tried to scam me out of money. I was emotionally devastated and felt victimized until I looked for the context of purpose. I asked myself, "What is the lesson I'm to learn from this?"

I went to a psychic for a tarot card reading. The important cards that emerged during my reading were the Strength card, which has an image of a woman taming a lion, and the Seven of Wands, which has an image of a man defending himself against attack. The reading was clear, though I didn't like the answer. I needed to be strong and confront the situation. At that time I hated confrontation, so I kept searching for other answers as to what I should do, hoping that the reading was wrong.

I attended an "Oracle Workshop," in which I consulted the *Pythia*, the priestess of prophecy, for a message. "The only way to go is through it," the voice behind the curtain declared. But still I resisted.

The following day I received information about a spiritual tour to India. One of the highlights on the itinerary was the opportunity to see the avatar, or spiritual master, Sai Baba. I decided I would write a letter asking the holy man for advice and go on the tour to allow myself to literally place my situation in his hands.

A few days into the tour, while traveling on a train to Bangalore, I met a young German man who was traveling to another ashram. He was a numerologist, but it wasn't the typical kind of numerology practiced here. Since I was curious, he offered to do a reading for me. I didn't tell him my problem. The first thing he said was, "You need to develop backbone. Be strong and stand up for yourself. It's your purpose."

By the time I visited Sai Baba's ashram, I was clear on what I needed to do, for every time I'd asked for spiritual advice, I'd received the same message. I realized that the person who was trying to scam me thought he could do so because I am a sensitive soul. He would tease me and call me a flake because of my spiritual beliefs. To him, I was a pushover. He saw me as simply a hundred-pound weakling. I understood I had to sue him to gain my self-respect. It wasn't easy—I had never hired a lawyer before—but I did it. I uncovered inner resources I didn't know I had.

Exercise: Find Your Purpose

For this exercise, you'll need to write in your journal in a comfortable place where you won't be disturbed. Allow at least ten minutes to complete the exercise.

From where you are sitting, look around the room you are in and pick the first three things that attract your attention. Don't think about it too much. Just trust your first impression. Go with your instinct. Place the objects in front of you in a line from left to right.

Close your eyes. Go into a light trance by taking eight deep, connected breaths. When you feel calm and centered, open your eyes.

- The first object on the far left represents your purpose. It symbolizes what you really want in life—what you're looking for. Or if you already know what your purpose is, you can use this exercise to help find the purpose in any circumstance or challenge you are facing. Write the answers to the following questions in your journal:
    - If this object could talk, what would it say about your relationship to your purpose?
    - What is it about this object that attracts you? Why do you like it?
    - If you were this object, how would you see your life purpose?

  As you look inside yourself, the answer may come immediately. Trust what comes.

- The second object represents your block or resistance. Write the answers to the following questions in your journal:
    - If this object could talk, what would it say about your ability to be on track with your purpose?
    - If you were this object, how would you feel?

- Is there anything about this object that makes you uncomfortable?

- The third object represents the solution or a new approach you need to take to discover your purpose. Write the answers to the following questions in your journal:
  - If this object could talk, what would it tell you that others say about you?
  - What advice would this object give about how to treat others?
  - If you acted like this object, what would you do?
  Write down any insights you received.

Support for Your Purpose

Plants can be wonderful aids that help you connect with your purpose. I've incorporated the therapeutic qualities of flower essences in my soul-healing practice since the mid-eighties, and clients have had outstanding results.

Dr. Edward Bach, a British physician and scientist, pioneered the development of Bach Flower Remedies in the 1930s. Through extensive research, he discovered that each flower could help a specific emotional or mental condition.

Flowers have been used to express our emotions throughout history. We use them at weddings, celebrations, and holidays to express our joy. Sending flowers on Valentine's Day sends a message of love. A home-delivered bouquet may express an apology. A vase of flowers next to a person in a hospital bed sends a wish to recover. A spray sent to a funeral supports our grief and mourning.

Bach discovered that the flowers' vibrational imprints or subtle energies provided healing properties and worked in the same way as homeopathic medicines. Every flower species has a particular vibration different in some way than any other. Bach developed a system of using thirty-eight flowers native to Great Britain. American companies, such as Flower Essence Services and Pegasus Products, have also researched and developed new essences using native plants that grow in the United States. I've used them for more than two decades and have found them to be highly effective.

Commercial or homemade flower essences contain infinitesimal amounts of plant material. Flowers are picked at the peak of their blossoming and put in a glass bowl holding pure water. They are exposed to sunlight for about three hours. The flowers are then discarded, and the water is preserved with a small amount of brandy. The water's molecular structure is charged and imprinted with the soul pattern of the flowers' vibrational essence. It is this "plant signature" that heals.

The essences can help release emotional distress and self-defeating thought patterns. They aid in clearing problems such as indecision, fear, mental exhaustion, hopelessness, and more. Some have more than one benefit and can be used for several different purposes. They are nontoxic and nonaddictive, and can be used with other medications. It is better to take small amounts of a flower essence over a longer period of time for best results as opposed to taking it all at once.

You can buy flower essences commercially or make your own. When you begin taking an essence, you may become more aware of an unwanted pattern affecting your life. You may feel worse at first, for the pattern may become amplified in order to get your attention so that you can change it, but that will pass and you will experience positive change.

Using Flower Essences

I've labeled those developed by Bach (http://feelbach.com) and FES-Flower Essence Services (http://www.fesflowers.com). Scan the list, and trust your feeling about which essence calls out to you. I find that it is better to choose just one at first; that way you can get to know the individual remedy more intimately. Take small amounts of a flower essence for at least six weeks for best results. Two drops four times a day is an average dosage. Essences are taken under the tongue, in a glass of water, or can be rubbed behind the earlobes. Feel its unique effect and experience what it can do for you. Once you get to know the effects of a remedy, you can take up to five essences at one time.

Flower Essences for Your Purpose

Here is a list of commercially available essences that can help you find purpose in your life, recognize your self-worth, trust your inner wisdom, and manifest your goals.

- Blackberry helps one manifest goals. (FES)
- Buttercup helps one know one's true worth and accept one's destiny. (FES)
- Centaury helps one be of service to others, yet remain true to self. (Bach)
- Cerrato helps one trust one's inner wisdom. (Bach)
- Impatience can relieve stress on the heart caused by a frenetic lifestyle. (Bach)
- Lady's slipper aids one in contacting one's true purpose. (FES)
- Larch brings confidence to follow one's destiny. (Bach)
- Madia aids clarity of purpose. (FES)
- Scleranthus helps one overcome indecision and make choices. (Bach)
- Scotch broom motivates one to serve humanity. (FES)
- Walnut assists one in remaining true to one's destiny. (Bach)
- Wild oat helps one find clarity about one's life purpose. (Bach)

Commercial remedies are great to have on hand because it is not always possible to make the kind of remedy you need. The plant may not grow in your area or may not be in bloom. I've included resources at the end of the book to help you learn more about remedies.

Taking essences can help deepen your relationship with nature. I always teach my Reiki apprentices how to make an essence, for there is power in dealing directly with the plant.

Making a Flower Essence

Choose a sunny day to make your flower essence. Morning hours are preferable, before the heat of the day sets in. Ultimately, the best essences come from your garden or from flowers that grow wild in your backyard. Please note that public parks may have laws or regulations regarding picking flowers. If you are picking wildflowers, choose a nonpolluted area where the flowers are growing abundantly, and before you use any flower be certain that you have identified it correctly; if you are not completely sure, don't use it.

You will need the following items:

- a glass measuring cup
- scissors or a knife
- a small glass bowl
- tweezers
- a small bottle of spring water
- three one-ounce dropper bottles with stoppers
- labels and a pen
- a bottle of good brandy
- a pinch of tobacco or cornmeal

Step One: Making the Mother Elixir

A. Sterilize the measuring cup, scissors/knife, tweezers, and the glass bowl by dipping them into boiling water for a moment. Place these items in a bag, along with the bottle of spring water. You'll also need three one-ounce dropper bottles with stoppers, and labels and a pen. The brandy is used as a preservative, and the pinch of tobacco or cornmeal is a gift for the nature spirits. Take these items to your destination.

B. When you arrive, take your equipment out of the bag. Pour a half-cup of spring water into your bowl. A little goes a long way. Take a moment to tune yourself to the nature spirits. Make an offering of tobacco or cornmeal. With a receptive, reverent attitude, call upon the spirits of the plants. Thank them for their cooperation. Ask those plants who want to be part of the remedy to stand out; they will seem to pop out at you.

C. Clean-cut flowers (don't tear) with your sterilized scissors or knife. Staying true to the same species, choose from many plants if possible. Never pick an area clean. Allow the blossoms to fall into your sterilized bowl of spring water until the surface is totally covered with flowers.

D. Once filled, set the bowl in sunlight for two to four hours.

E. Afterward, pick off the flowers with tweezers, and give the flowers back to the earth to be recycled. Pour the water into a glass stopper bottle until it is half full. Add an equal amount of brandy. This is the mother elixir. Label the bottle with the name of the flower, the words "Mother Elixir," and the date. This elixir will last for seven years.

If you have any leftover water, you can repeat the process and make another bottle for a friend or pour the excess flower water back on your garden and gift it back to the plants.

Step Two: Making the Stock Bottle

F. Pour a teaspoon of brandy, to be used as a preservative, into a one-ounce dropper bottle. Fill it with spring water. Add two drops of the mother elixir. This becomes the stock bottle. Label it with the name of the flower essence, the words "Stock Bottle," and the date. This stock mixture will last for seven years.

Step Three: Making the Dosage Bottle

G. Pour a teaspoon of brandy, to be used as a preservative, into a one-ounce dropper bottle. Fill it with spring water. Add two drops from the stock bottle. This is the dosage bottle. Label it with the name of the flower essence, the words "Dosage Bottle," and the date. This dosage mixture will expire in six weeks.

H. Once the dosage bottle is completed, you can take two to four drops from it four times a day or as needed. Drops can be taken directly under the tongue or put into a glass of water. You can also apply the flower essence topically or in bathwater.

Whether you make your own or buy them commercially, taking flower essences is like having a personal support team. Their healing is powerful, yet very gentle. The flowers generously give themselves to serve humanity with love.

Being Purposeful

Now that you are in touch with your life purpose, have a personal code to live by, and have help from the plants, life takes on a greater ease. If you have been practicing the niyamas, you have begun to find your purpose in every situation. You've probably noticed some subtle changes happening. Or perhaps others have been complimenting you lately for your ability to be more patient, thoughtful, or positive. Your health may have improved if you have been practicing saucha, cleanliness. Or if you've been practicing santosh, you may feel more content with what you have, so you are less stressed. By incorporating flower essences to your daily routine, you have added a new community of support to your spiritual growth. Every one of these methods will help strengthen the others and support your continued spiritual growth.

Chapter Six

CHOOSE CLARITY

Knowing what you want is the first step to obtaining it. In this chapter, you'll connect to your inner wisdom to discover what is truly important to you. The exercises and meditations will help you gain clarity and ground your intentions by placing them in a time frame. The stories will empower you to take control and steer the course of your life. You'll learn how to apply the Karmic Intentions Formula to create a life of your dreams.

The Law of Attraction

You are a creative being, manifesting your experience of life continually throughout each day. Some desired results are easy to produce quickly. For example, you're upset because of dealing with a challenging situation and need to talk to someone. You reach out and text a few friends, but no one seems to be available. Just when you're ready to believe that no one cares, a friend miraculously calls you. But other times, matters seem to take more time and effort to resolve. For instance, maybe you want a loving partner or satisfying work and need to be patient for the process to unfold.

The law of attraction has become very popular since the film *The Secret* debuted in 2006. Esther Hicks, an American inspirational speaker and best-selling author, has also brought the law of attraction to the mainstream by channeling an entity called Abraham. However, the law of attraction is not new, for it has ancient roots in hermetic magic and is written about in the classic occult book *The Kybalion*. The same principles of this law are also at work in astrology; the planet Venus in your horoscope can reveal your style of attracting things to you as well as if there are afflictions that hinder you getting what you want.

The law of attraction states that you attract to yourself that which you hold inside you. Like attracts like. The law of attraction is in operation all the time, so whatever you see in your life—the good and bad—is a reflection of your beliefs as well as your past actions. By using this law consciously with intent, you can attract everything you want or need by thinking about it and maintaining a positive emotional state.

However, your conscious thoughts must be in alignment with your unconscious mind. If you want a loving relationship but deep down believe you are unlovable, you will not be able to attract a sustainable mate. Or if you want to be rich but unconsciously believe that money is the root of evil, you will hit roadblocks to your financial success. You need to keep clearing out subconscious baggage in order to maintain alignment with your conscious mind, your unconscious mind, and your Higher Self.

But some people misunderstand the law of attraction. Some believe that if they just know what they want and write affirmations or make a treasure map, their dreams will come true. This faulty belief is called *magical thinking*, because most often you need to take actions toward furthering your goals. If you want to win the lottery, you need to buy a ticket. If you want to have a loving relationship, it helps if you socialize so you can meet new people. Prince Charming isn't likely to just show up on your doorstep. You have to be actively engaged in the game of life.

Whatever the case, manifesting an intended result follows a simple formula, as you can see enacted in Joan's story.

Joan's Story

Joan needed transportation to get to work at the beauty salon on the weekends. Finding a parking space in the city was difficult, so she ruled out driving. Taking the bus was unreliable, since the bus didn't seem to run on schedule. So Joan decided that a road bicycle would be the right solution.

Once she made up her mind that a bike would be the best option, she fantasized about the kind of bike she wanted and could see it clearly in her mind's eye. Her blue recumbent bike would be light and sleek with a streamline seat. She'd be able to carry its lightweight aluminum frame out of her apartment and onto the street by herself.

However, when Joan called several bicycle shops in her area, she was disappointed by the response from shopkeepers: "You'll never find what you're looking for. We're sold out. It's the end of the season." Joan even searched the Internet, but had no luck.

Being determined, Joan said to herself, "I want that bike, and I am going to have it." It was autumn, and cold weather was approaching. She didn't want to stand outside in the cold waiting for a bus. She needed the bike within the next two weeks.

The following day, she saw an ad for a bike shop in her neighborhood. When she got there, the store was closed. Suddenly, like a lightning flash, she thought, *There's a pawnshop around the corner.* In that moment, she knew that she would get her bike and that she would get it at a huge discount. But she had no idea how she knew it would happen. She had never even been to a pawnshop before.

When Joan arrived at the pawnshop, she asked the clerk if there were any road bikes available for sale. The clerk said, "Yes, I believe we have something that sounds like what you are looking for."

Joan followed the clerk down a flight of stairs into a dark, dank basement. A blue lightweight recumbent bike, just like what Joan had been visualizing, was leaning against the wall in the corner.

Joan was so surprised when she saw the bike, she rubbed her eyes as she thought, *No—it couldn't be.*

The clerk carried the bike upstairs into the lighted shop. Joan's mouth opened in astonishment. It was the exact model she wanted, the right color, the perfect size, and in mint condition. When the clerk said it cost only one hundred dollars, Joan was so amazed that she couldn't get her wallet out of her purse fast enough. She was getting what she wanted for only a fraction of the cost.

Using the Karmic Intentions Formula

Let's look at the manifestation process using Joan's story as an example.

1. Creation starts as a ***desire***. Look at the big picture. Joan needed reliable transportation to get to work and decided a bicycle would be her best option.

2. She developed ***clarity*** on what kind of bike she wanted. It's important to be specific.

3. Next, Joan set an ***intention.*** She decided she would acquire the bike.

4. Joan had an intended ***time frame***. She needed the bike by the end of the month.

5. Next, she took ***action*** to achieve her objective. She visited local shops and searched the Internet.

6. Using ***determination***, Joan kept going and did not give up on her goal, even though she thought she'd exhausted her resources.

7. Finally, the ***price*** was right. The value of the bike was in agreement with the value Joan was willing to pay.

We will go over these simple steps to manifesting what you want in detail in this chapter.

1. Desires: True and False

I've heard many people say, "I want to be independently wealthy so I can just spend my life lying on the beach." Well, I talked to a woman who runs a jewelry shop on a Caribbean island who said that she once thought that too. She moved to the island to get away from big city pressures and thought she would find escape from life through lounging on pink sand and floating in turquoise waters for the rest of her days.

"After two months, I got really bored," she admitted. What she thought she wanted wasn't what she truly wanted at all. But now she has found true happiness making jewelry in a beautiful environment. She gets pleasure from selling her work to someone, for she knows she has contributed to bringing more beauty and enjoyment into another's life.

Contained in every desire is the seed of creation. Knowing what you want is the first step in having it. And placing your desire in a larger context can help you achieve it. So if you have a want, it's best to first look at the bigger picture.

In Joan's case, she needed transportation that worked, so getting a bicycle was a result out of that context. She didn't want a bicycle just to have one; the bike had a purpose. So if you want to lose five pounds, the bigger picture might be to have a healthy lifestyle. If your objective is to just lose the weight, chances are you would gain it back again and get caught in a vicious cycle of losing and gaining weight. However, if you live out of a context of a healthy lifestyle, you are more apt to make transformational changes that have longer-lasting results.

The more specific you are, the easier it is for the universe to give you what you want. When you go to a restaurant, you order something from the menu. It is unlikely that you would tell the waitress to just bring anything. If that were the case, you'd have a fifty-fifty chance of being satisfied. But sometimes what you desire may not yet be clear when the waitress asks you what you want. When confronted with too many choices it is easy to feel overwhelmed, so you choose something you enjoyed in the past, which may or may not be satisfying. Or you may feel adventurous and order something new on the menu, which could turn out to be a great discovery or complete flop. You have to be in the mood for a risk, because you may have a disappointing experience and end up feeling you didn't get your money's worth. Or maybe you are out of touch with what your body needs, so you order the wrong thing and wind up regretting it later, suffering from indigestion.

2. Clarifying What You Want

Here's a simple process to help you get in touch with what you want. Let's use "I want a healthy body" as an example, but you can make up your own category.

Step one is to write your intent on the top of a clean page in your journal.

Step two is to make a list of what you know you don't want. For instance, if you are ordering at a restaurant and don't know what you want, your list may look like this:

- I don't want a high-calorie lunch.

- I don't want to eat junk food.

- I don't want to feel heavy and sleepy after eating.

- I don't want something rich.

- I don't want to eat a big portion.

Next, turn the negative traits into positive ones to get a clear picture of what you do want. Write at least a paragraph in your journal. It might sound something like this:

> I want a nourishing, healthy, low-calorie lunch. Something light and easily digestible would be best, because I'll be sitting all afternoon. I have to work, so I want something that will give me energy but not so much that I'll feel restless. Since I don't need a big portion, I'll go with the soup and salad.

The task of writing a paragraph may inspire you to learn more about what you want. Embellish your paragraph with more qualities you discover. The paragraph could be about anything you want: job, home, car, etc. How many pages can you fill discovering what you want? If you could have anything you wanted, what would it be?

What is the big picture? If it is money you want, why do you want it? Is it because you'd like financial freedom so you could focus on your creative talents? How would you use your money to make the world a better place?

Explore all the categories. The sky is the limit. Let yourself go. The following exercise can help you get your creative juices flowing as you focus on what you want to have, be, and do.

Exercise:
Having, Being, Doing

Sometimes we sell ourselves short by listening to our automatic response that says, "I can't afford that" or "I don't have time to do that," so instead of consciously creating life, we fall into the trap of reacting to circumstances. The television commercial's slogan "Life comes at you fast" sums it up rather well. This exercise will help you get in touch with what you want.

Just for fun, imagine that you had all the time and money you needed to accomplish your goals.

Title one page of your journal "100 Things I Want to Have," title the next page "100 Things I Want to Be," and title the next page "100 Things I Want to Do."

Next, fill in your lists. If you run out of wants before you reach one hundred, then go back to this process each day and write a few more until the lists are complete. Or maybe you find it hard to think of so many things because you want *big* things. Perhaps you have so much that you may need to instead create lists of accomplishments you can give to the world.

Flower Essences Can Help You Gain Clarity

Here is a list of essences that can help you cut through confusion. Please refer to the section Using Flower Essences in chapter five for dosage information.

- Deerbrush can help connect you to your inner truth. (FES)
- Dill releases feelings of overwhelm caused by too many unintegrated experiences. (FES)
- Madia helps focus intentions. (FES)
- Mullein helps clarify one's moral values. (FES)
- Rabbitbrush helps one see the bigger picture. (FES)
- White chestnut brings mental clarity. (Bach)
- Wild oat brings clarity of one's life purpose. (Bach)

Record in your journal what essences you choose to take. Take note of how they help you gain clarity in your life. You may want to create an affirmation to say out loud when you take your essence. Note if you have emotions that come to the surface as part of the clearing process. Do you have quick results with this essence? Or do you need to take another essence to get at a deeper issue?

3. Setting an Intention by Treasure Mapping

Once you have clarity on what you want, create an intention. Write it in your journal.

Forming an intention will help you focus your energy on what is important. You will then organize your time to bring your vision into reality.

Imagery is a powerful tool to crystalize your intentions. This process will help you develop your power to manifest by making a collage of what you want. You'll need a sheet of blank paper (any size), scissors, a glue stick, and a few old magazines for this process.

- Give your project a title. It may be something like "Rolling in Dough," "Twin Flames," or "House Beautiful." Have the title be inspiring and appealing.

- Tear out images in magazines that resonate with your desired outcome. For example, if you want a relationship, you may find pictures of lovers holding hands while walking on the beach. As you go through magazines, try not to think too much. If the image grabs you when you see it, use it. You can also add words or slogans, such as "You can do it!"

- When you have enough pictures to fill your paper, begin gluing them together in a collage.

- If you are feeling creative, you may want to photocopy the Magician card. Replace his head with a photo of your face. Glue it to the center of your collage.

- Display your "Treasure Map" in a prominent place in your home. I always pin mine to my bulletin board in my office, where I see it every day.

Testing Your Intention Meditation

When you have a clear intention of what you want, use the following meditation to see if you are on the right track. Go to a private space where you won't be disturbed. You may want to record this meditation ahead of time so that you can be fully in the process.

Begin recording the following script:

Relax into a comfortable position. Close your eyes and focus on your breath. Begin to let go of any tension you are holding in your body. Allow your eyes to drop away from your eyelids. Release your tongue ... your jaw ... your neck. Just let go. You feel a sense of lightness, a sense of peace and oneness.

Imagine you are on stage in front of a huge audience composed of your dearest friends, your spirit guides, and guardian angels that love you unconditionally. They want to see you be fulfilled and truly happy. Off to the left is a teleprompter screen.

You're going to let the audience decide whether you are on the right track. By listening to the amount of enthusiasm in their applause, you'll know whether to pursue your intention at this time.

State out loud your intention of what you want.

Listen to the applause. Trust what comes.

Now look up at the teleprompter to the left. Receive a message written out in bright lights on the screen.

What does it say?

When you feel as though you've received your advice, slowly open your eyes and come back to your normal waking state.

End your recording.

Write down your experience in your journal. What was the response from the audience? Was it a wild, enthusiastic roar? Did you get a standing ovation? Did you hear a mild show of support? Did you get booed off the stage?

What did the written message say?

If the response was positive and you know you are ready to move forward, proceed with the following exercises. If you are not on the right path, choose another intention and repeat the process. Keep repeating with different intention until you know you have found a intention worth pursuing.

4. Setting a Time Frame

Intentions without specific time lines are not likely to be achieved. Instead of being manifested into a reality, they fall into the category of wishful thinking or fantasy. There is no power to achieve a result. Someday it will happen—but someday never comes.

For example, you run into an old friend on the street. You are delighted to see her. You chat for a few minutes. Before you depart and go on with your day, you say, "Let's have lunch sometime." Your friend smiles and nods in agreement, and then you say your good-byes. But your lunch date never happens because you are drawn into the next circumstance of the day. And in a day or so, you forget you even mentioned having lunch.

If you really wanted to make a lunch date, your conversation would go something like this:

"Let's have lunch."

"That would be great. I'm free next Tuesday. Are you available?"

"Perfect. What time?"

"Is noon okay?"

"Fine. Where should we go?"

"How about the Hot Spot Café?"

"Great."

Phone numbers or e-mail addresses are exchanged so you can confirm your date. You place the date in your appointment calendar and set an alarm as a reminder. And the lunch date is most likely to happen.

Exercise:
Karmic Timing

For this exercise, you'll need to write the answers to the following questions on a clean page in your journal.

What is your intention for your life? What do you want to achieve? How long will it take to achieve it? Be realistic. Pie-in-the-sky expectations only bring disappointment and disempowerment. Break it down into measureable times. Where do you want to be in ten years? Five years? Two years? One year?

What is your short-term intention? Where do you want to be in six months? Two months? One month? One week?

Look at your calendar and create specific dates to track your progress. For example, if you wanted to lose five pounds over the next three months, you would want to be at least two and a half pounds lighter in forty-five days. This is a way to measure how well you are doing. In twenty days you would need to be at least one pound lighter.

5. Taking Action

After you have scheduled a realistic time frame to work toward your intention, think of the actions you will need to take to make it a reality. It is best to break actions down into simple steps. Write down three simple steps that will further you toward manifesting your intention.

If you are someone who knows you'll have trouble following through with your actions, ask a friend to hold you accountable. Schedule coaching calls to support each other. A five-minute conversation at the end of the day can work wonders. It could go something like this:

Your coach asks you, "Did you do what you'd committed to doing today?"

If you did, go on to retarget what you are going to do for the next day or week, and schedule your follow-up call.

If you did not, declare that. Just state the facts without adding guilt, shame, or bad feelings. Retarget and set your actions for the next day or week. Schedule your follow-up call.

What other structures can you add to support your intention? For example, if you want to exercise, you may want to buy DVDs with routines to follow at home. But if you know you lack the discipline needed to work out by yourself, you may want to sign up for fitness classes.

Are there other people you can add to your support team? List people who can help because of the expertise and resources they offer. How can you gain their support?

6. Determination

You can be sure that once you declare an intention and are in action, obstacles will surface to test your commitment. You may encounter your own negative thoughts trying to sabotage you. For example, if you are in sales and want to increase your income, your mind may want to put off out-reaching to others by saying, "I'll start tomorrow." If your intention is to start exercising, you may hear your mind say, "I don't feel like doing this," as it is time to leave for your Pilates class. Or "just one piece of cake won't matter" may try to hinder your desire to lose weight as you peruse the desert menu.

Unforeseen circumstances may try to throw you off track. An unexpected expense—the car breaks down, your pet gets sick and needs to go to the vet, you crack your tooth—may drain your budget, taking away resources you were counting on using.

Sometimes changes in the circumstances of people in your life affect you. Your babysitter tells you she's moving across the country, so you are suddenly left without child-care; therefore, you no longer have extra time set aside for you. Or your coworker quits, leaving you to do double the workload in the office, so you come home exhausted with no energy to devote to your goal. Or your elderly parent gets sick, and the free slots in your schedule are taken up as you are cast into the role of caretaker.

When circumstances become obstacles, the important thing to remember is to be persistent. You may need to adjust your time frame and reshuffle your priorities, but determination is important. Many famous authors—including Stephen King, Tony Hillerman, and J. K. Rowling—were rejected numerous times before their books were published. Many sports teams have had losing streaks before they got back on top again. Even famous actors have had ups and downs in their careers. Be unstoppable. Don't give up, or you'll never get there.

7. The Price You Pay

Everything has a price—your home, relationships, career, and possessions. Sometimes the price is obvious; other times, there are hidden costs. Some things are a bargain; other things are overpriced. Sometimes the cost is a bartered exchange.

Even things that appear to be free are always paid for in some way, whether it's with money, time, or sweat. Other times the fee is an emotional investment or a sacrifice. For instance, if you want to be a parent, you have to be willing to make personal sacrifices for your child, for babies need a lot of time and attention.

American society has paid a high price for modern conveniences. Exploitation in any form has karmic consequences that perpetuate suffering. Industries have polluted rivers and streams. Corporations have gone to the third world to hire

cheap labor, creating sweatshops and unfair working conditions—and many Americans have lost their jobs in the
process.

Your personal values determine whether something is
worth the cost. Values are your fundamental beliefs of what
is important to you. They influence decisions about right or
wrong, should or shouldn't, and good or bad. They also affect
your ability to manifest your intentions, for your values must
be in alignment with your goals.

For instance, say you want to increase your income so that
you can buy a BMW. But you unconsciously believe that it
isn't okay to flaunt your wealth because others will be jeal-
ous and hate you. You will probably not be able to afford to
buy things that show your status until you let go of that belief. Something will hold you back.

Your family, country, religion, education, and the news
media influence your personal values. Some values you inherit unconsciously; others you choose purposefully. But if
you haven't clearly defined them and consciously decided
which ones are the most important to you, then it's easy to
feel that you have less control over the choices you make.

Every family has different values. Some are clannish and
stick together. Others are spread out all over the country.
Some families believe that the rituals of eating at sit-down
dinners together and sharing are important, while others
chow down on the run. Some families believe in full-blown,
honest communication, while others are secretive and private. A strong work ethic may run in your family, or maybe

you were raised to be an epicurean with the belief that life should be devoted to pleasure.

Core values play a large role in your job satisfaction. Some people need personal freedom and variety in their job, while others prefer a regular routine. Some people like a high-stress job that compensates with a large salary, while others prefer to work in a laid-back atmosphere that brings high emotional satisfaction but has lower monetary compensation. If you have a conflict between your core values and the values you're being asked to assume by your employer, eventually you will dread going to work.

Your country also influences your values. Americans love freedom, so much so that living in this society presents thousands of choices to be made each day. We have a huge selection of cable and Internet channels to watch, a variety of foods available to eat, and a large range of items to buy. Technology has expanded our choices beyond what is natural so that we can become pregnant even if we are infertile, live in an inhospitable desert environment with air conditioning, or even change gender. Gun control is a hot topic because we want to have the right to bear arms even though mass shootings are on the rise.

It is essential to be clear on what your values are so you can spend your life doing things that are meaningful to you. If you know what is most important to you, you can make better choices as to whom you want to partner with in romance, friendship, and business. You'll have a better understanding of what kind of job to take or in what neighborhood to buy your home. The following exercise can help you gain clarity on what is most important to you.

Exercise:
Karmic Price Tags

Step One: Core Values

Title a blank page in your journal "My Core Values." Answer the following questions:

- What is important to you?

- What does money mean to you?

- What does success mean to you in your career?

- What does success mean to you in a relationship?

Step Two: Inherited Values

For this part of exercise, you'll need to write down the answers to the questions on a clean page in your journal.

Give yourself time to think about what is really important to you in all the categories. Feel free to add categories of your own.

What values did you inherit from your family in regard to the following areas?

- how you express your personal appearance

- how you take care of your body

- owning things

- maintaining what you have

- financial security

- learning and education
- the kind of car you drive
- the type of house you live in
- the type of neighborhood you live in
- family life
- having children
- how you relate to your children
- your daily rituals: eating, relaxing, tending to your chores, etc.
- your work
- your romantic relationships or mate
- sex
- participating in a religious community
- your health habits and how you take care of yourself
- filing taxes
- your career
- having access to clean air and water
- self-expression
- your friendships
- taking vacations

After you complete the categories, go over them again and ask what you've inherited from your country, your religion, your education, and the news media. You may find that some values are outdated and no longer serve you. You may find that you've absorbed someone else's value, but it isn't really yours. Take a moment to see how your current life, work, and relationships reflect your core values. Is your lifestyle in alignment with what is really important to you? Write down your observations.

Exercise:
Self-Worth Tips

How you value yourself also affects your ability to have what you want. If deep down inside you feel unworthy, you won't be able to be satisfied. Valuing your time, being kind and gentle with yourself, and affirming your highest qualities can help build self-love. Take a few minutes to write in your journal the top ten things you love about yourself. Then write ten things you can do to make your life more pleasurable. Write affirmations that assert that you deserve to have what you want.

Exercise:
Arrogance

The opposite of low self-esteem is arrogance, which is an inflated sense of self-importance. Those who believe they are better than others often feel they deserve more than their fair share and have an excessive feeling of personal entitlement. This deadly sin can cause even more harm than feeling undeserving, for it can lead to criminal behavior or legal disputes. You can see examples of this in the news on a regular basis—politicians who take public funds for personal use, or priests who sexually abuse parishioners' children. Personal entitlement issues are also common themes on courtroom television. Oftentimes a person who has borrowed money from a friend or romantic partner doesn't feel obligated to pay it back and justifies it by feeling entitled to it.

Take a few minutes to write in your journal where you feel personally entitled. Where do you see the negative effects of entitlement in the world? How can you make a difference in those areas? In what situations do you need to show more humility?

Exercise: Buying It

Once you're clear on what you want and why you want it, and you have a time frame set and a three-step action plan, the next step is to consider how your intention will affect your community.

Step One: Your Intention

Make your intention the title on a clean sheet of paper in your journal. Write down the answers to the following questions:

- Is your intention good for you? Explain why.

- Is your intention good for others? Explain why.

- Is your intention good for the planet? Explain why.

- Is your intention good in the long or short term? Explain why.

- Do you know the full price of what you'll pay in time, sweat, or money to pursue your intention?

- If not, is there someone who could advise you?
- What are the hidden costs?
- How much will it cost to maintain?
- Are you willing to pay the price of obtaining it?

- How will your life change if you create this? What are some actions that you'll need to take to accomplish it?

- Do you feel you deserve to have this?

- Does it fit in with your current values, or will you have to stretch outside your value system?

Step Two: Are You Ready?

- If you determine your intention is good for you and everyone, and you're willing to pay the price, list at least five negative words or phrases that describe your resistance to the price you have to pay for your project. For example, let's say you're in sales and your intention is to make nine thousand dollars in new sales this month, but you don't like cold calling and want to resist doing it; the associated negative responses may be *burden, bothersome, intrusive, confrontational,* and *hate to hear "no."* Write down what you resist.

- Now, turn those negative qualities into possibilities. For instance, the negative connotations about cold calling could be transformed by viewing the interaction as a positive opportunity:
    - an invitation for people to connect with me
    - a chance to make a difference in someone's life

- an opportunity to contribute
- a chance to share my talents

Your Inner Magician Meditation

For this meditation, you'll need a deck of Rider-Waite tarot cards. If you don't have one, search the Magician tarot card image online. Focus on it until you can recall it in your mind's eye. Once you have a sense of what this card looks like, proceed with the following meditation. You may want to record it so that you can be fully in the process.

Begin recording the following script:

Go into a state of relaxation by taking a few deep, connected breaths.

Imagine the Magician card in your mind's eye growing larger and larger until the figure becomes life-size. Step into the card.

Once you've entered the card, experience yourself in a garden. Red roses and white lilies are in full bloom. The rose petals are like velvet, while the light on the lilies makes it appear that they are glowing. When you inhale the scent of their delicate perfume, you feel slightly intoxicated by their fragrance.

The magician stands before you, wearing a white tunic covered by a red robe. Feel the love and kindness emanating from his eyes. You feel safe and happy to be in his presence, for he is a wise, evolved being.

The magician knows everything about you, even your deepest desires. Take a moment and ask him, "What should I focus on at this point in my life?"

Allow the response to just flow into your mind. Trust what comes.

The magician picks up the magic wand from the table and places it in your hand. You feel a surge of power fill your being, and you know you have the ability to create what you want. You can direct your life on a course that is filled with passion, love, satisfaction, abundance, and contribution. Take a moment to feel the power you have to create your life. What is it that you want?

Set the wand back on the table and take up the cup—the symbol of your emotions. How will your new reality feel? If it's a loving relationship you desire, how will it feel to have a partner? What body sensations are connected to this feeling? Pay attention to what is happening in your heart. Do you feel afraid? Excited? Are there butterflies in your stomach? Do you feel something else?

If it's a new home you want, how will it feel to have a private sanctuary where you are renewed and restored? Imagine how much fun it will be to decorate it. How will it feel to entertain family and friends? Will you plant a garden?

If it's a new job you are after, imagine yourself enjoying your work. Visualize yourself being happy, knowing you are making a difference by being there. See yourself making and saving more money than ever before. New possibilities open up because of this. You are able to do more things that you enjoy.

Or if it's something else you desire, imagine having it now. Feel the joy, the fun, the satisfaction …

Now set down the cup and take hold of the sword—the symbol of your thoughts. Believe it is possible to have what you desire. Take a moment to affirm that you deserve to have what you want! Believe it can happen.

Now set down the sword and take hold of the wand— the symbol of action and will. Feel your desire burning with a driving passion. Commit to taking action toward achieving your goal. Affirm that you have the drive to persist even when the going gets tough. Know that you have the endurance and stamina to keep going even when your goal seems unachievable.

Now put the wand back in its spot and pick up the coin. Are you willing to pay the price to have what you want? If it's love you want, you may need to learn how to be vulnerable. You may have to develop in new ways to be a good partner. You may need to learn how to compromise or be supportive. It will not be easy all the time. Because no one is perfect, you will have to deal with your partner's negative traits. Can you be patient? Forgiving? Caring? You may be hurt in the process; are you willing to take that chance? Can you risk being rejected? Look and see if you are willing to pay the price.

If it's a home that you are wanting, are you willing to pay the monthly mortgage payment? Will it be stressful to come up with extra money each month? Can you afford to pay the taxes on it? Are you willing to maintain your property? Will you take care to see that it is cleaned, insured, and repaired? You will become part of a community by buying a house; are you willing to be a good neighbor? Look and see if you are willing to pay the price.

If it's a better job you want, are you willing to seek out better employment? You may need to rewrite your résumé or take a class to catch up on the latest technology in your field. Are you willing to face your competition? Are you willing to risk failing? It can be emotionally confrontational to take on this challenge; are you willing to step out of your comfort zone? What are the hidden costs? Look and see if you are willing to pay the price.

The magician is witnessing your every step, and you feel supported.

If you are willing to pay the price for what you want, affirm that you will commit to the time and effort as you place the coin back on the table.

The magician hands you his special wand. Notice how elegant it is and how it differs from the one on the table. Hold it in your right hand, pointing it up to heaven. Point your left hand toward the earth. Feel a surge of power entering your wand as you align your personal will with divine will. Allow your deepest wish to take form. Thy will be done, or something better will come into your life.

Know you will achieve your goal at the right time.

Thank the magician. He smiles and says, "You can keep the wand."

Step out of the card. When you do, it shrinks back into its normal size.

End your recording.

Write down your experience in your journal. What was the message from the magician? What do you want? Could you feel it? Do you believe you can have it? Write a positive statement, affirming you can have it.

Do you know what actions you need to take to get what you want? Are you willing to take those actions? What are they? Write them down.

Are you willing to pay the price?

What is the biggest challenge you are going to have to deal with?

How will you have to stretch who you are to have what you want?

Karmic Intentions Formula Recap

Here's a recap of the manifestation process:

1. Creation starts as a **desire.** Look at the big picture, the context of your desire. What purpose do you need to fulfill?

2. Get **clarity** on what you want and whether you are willing to have it.

3. Once you are clear in your desire, set an **intention.**

4. Next, schedule a **time frame** in which your intention will manifest. How long will it take? Days? Months? Years?

5. What are the **actions** you need to take to initiate the process? Name three simple steps you can take within the week toward achieving your aim. Be determined.

If you cannot do it on your own, find a friend to support you in being accountable.

6. Is your ***determination*** strong? Are you willing to keep going, regardless of obstacles that present themselves, and not give up on your goal?

7. Examine the cost. Is what you want in alignment with your values? Is it good not only for yourself but also for your community and the planet? See if you are willing to pay the ***price***.

Now that you know how to use the Karmic Intentions Formula, you can apply it to create the life of your dreams. Each time you do, you will become clearer and clearer on what you truly want and what is most important to you. You will learn more about yourself and how to utilize your talents for the highest good. As you master the formula, your life will take on a sense of ease. You'll become more confident that you are working with karmic law to minimize negative karmic consequences. By constantly training yourself to actively use the Karmic Intention Formula, you will find that, after time, using it will become second nature, and as a result, you'll be more productive and fulfilled.

Chapter Seven

CHOOSE ACTION

Many people think they want something, but deep down they don't believe they can have it. Sometimes unconscious limiting beliefs can sabotage our endeavors. Or when things don't turn out as planned, we're thrown off course. However, when we are aligned with our soul's purpose, our course of action unfolds naturally. In this chapter, you will clear any resistance to having what you want, learning techniques to help you become unstuck and make changes with ease.

Your Resistance

Some people know what they want but have barriers to receiving it because of past conditioning. As a child, if you are constantly told by your parents or authority figures that you can't have what you want, the repeated suggestion is likely to take root in your unconscious and turn into a limiting belief. "I can't get what I want" becomes your automatic way of responding to circumstances. Conscious choice is not available, so the past colors your future. This pattern can be seen in Michelle's story.

When Michelle was a young child, she loved to sit on her mother's lap. The scent of her mother's perfume was delightful, and she felt safe being enveloped in her arms. But one summer day, while sitting with her mom on the sofa, she pulled at the pearl necklace that was circling her mother's throat, nearly breaking the strand. When her mother slapped her hand and scolded, "You can't have that," Michelle decided that she couldn't get what she wanted. It was as though she was given a sentence by a judge and jury. That decision became a limiting belief that colored her life for twenty years. It became her automatic way of being that influenced many of her decisions, and she was unaware of it.

As an adult, when Michelle would go to a restaurant, she never ordered what she really wanted but instead got the cheapest entrée on the menu. She never bought the designer clothes she longed to wear, instead filling her closet full of imitation knockoffs. As a result, she never felt confident in her appearance. She would justify her actions by saying, "I don't need that" or "I can't afford it," even though she could. She wanted to take a cooking class, but she never signed up because she thought she didn't have the time. She always found reasons and excuses to hold back.

Satisfaction wasn't present most of the time, for she was always settling for less. She felt resigned and cynical. Life did not occur to her to be an exciting adventure; instead, it was just a chain of unending compromises. Fortunately, a friend recommended Michelle get a tarot reading. When we began to uncover the source of the problem, her life took a turn for the better.

Exercise:
Gaining Insight

Take a moment to think about those situations in which you do not have what you want. Use the categories below to help you pinpoint specific areas that aren't working as well as you'd like.

- good body image
- nourishing diet
- possessions that make you feel comfortable and secure
- peaceful home environment
- recreation
- satisfying work
- friendships that nurture you
- financial security
- satisfying sex life
- active social life
- supportive family relationships
- transportation that serves you
- warm, loving relationships
- opportunities to contribute and make a difference

- travel and adventure

- fun and entertainment

What do you notice about having what you want? What areas need work or adjustments?

What are you attracting in all areas of your life? What are the conscious results you are producing? What are the unintentional results you are manifesting? In other words, what are you attracting that is unpleasant? What are you struggling with? What are your top challenges? Write down any insights you have in your journal.

Getting Even

Another kind of resistance to having what you want is rebellion, which is a form of self-sabotage. When we can't get what we want, the tendency is to get angry. It is easy to seek revenge out of frustration. "I'll show him" or "I'll get even" become a life sentence. Take Dan Wei's case, for instance.

Xiao Feng and Dan Wei had a special father-son bond and were rarely without each other. Dan Wei accompanied his dad during the day as his father renovated old apartments and in the evening when he watched movies with friends.

Xiao Feng wanted his son to be successful. He would frequently tell Dan Wei, "One day, you will do something huge for the world," instilling him with a hunger to achieve.

Dan Wei, wanting to please his dad, was driven to be an excellent student. He got As in calculus while in eighth grade. Later, he competed in national math contests and achieved such high rankings that he was able to take college credits during the summers while still in high school. Dan Wei had a sense of accomplishment and direction.

But just as Dan Wei's life was soaring upward, Xiao Feng was diagnosed with stage-four liver cancer. "Dan Wei, I am dying. You will have to take care of your mother and brothers when I die," Xiao Feng told his son.

Dan Wei, a teenager, was devastated when his father died. His anger at God simmered. He was also mad at his father for leaving him. He felt abandoned and alone. Unable to deal with his feelings, he became depressed. His grades dropped from As to Cs. When Dan Wei showed his mother his report card, tears fell from her eyes as she said, "Dan Wei, I am ashamed of you. What am I going to tell your father when I see him in the spirit world?"

Dan Wei became livid. He was outraged by his mother's unsupportive remark. All of the anger he'd bottled up inside seemed to explode, so he punched a hole in the living room wall. He was so filled with self-hatred, he said to himself, "I'll give you something to be ashamed of, Mother."

From then on, Dan Wei's life took a downward spiral. He made friends with the wrong crowd and spent his free time partying instead of studying. He cut classes because he was too tired from staying out late. He earned his first F in the twelfth grade. He managed to still get into a prestigious university, but he was kicked out his sophomore year.

Fortunately, fate intervened. Dan Wei met a kung fu master who changed his life by setting him on a spiritual path. Dan Wei began to take responsibility for his choices. He forgave himself, his parents, and God. He asked his mother to forgive him for his bad behavior as well. And now, a few years later, he is graduating from nursing school with honors. He has a close relationship with his mother, and his life is on the upswing again.

If you believe anger and resentment have been blocking your success, try practicing the following meditation.

Forgiveness Meditation

Perform this meditation in a private space where you won't be disturbed. It's best to make an audio recording of this ahead of time. Take a couple of minutes to pause after each question to allow enough time for the information to come through to you during the meditation. Don't rush. The whole process should take about fifteen minutes.

Begin recording the following script:

Relax into a comfortable position. Close your eyes and take a deep breath. Feel your breath move through your body like a gentle wave. When you inhale, inhale peace. Now exhale, and let go of any tension. Continue breathing deeply this way for a minute or two as you release all your concerns of the day. There's nowhere to get to, nothing to do but to be in the present moment.

Begin to feel a sense of lightness, a sense of peace and oneness. Enjoy this delicious moment of relaxation.

Imagine yourself sitting at home in your favorite chair. You feel safe and comfortable. Go within and ask your inner awareness these questions:

- Who do you need to forgive for blocking you from having what you want? You can recall the memory in a way that is easy and comfortable.

- Are you able to recall the incident? How old are you? Who are all the people involved?

- What decision did you make?

- What was the life sentence you created?

- Are you ready to release it?

- Where is this issue located in your body? Give it a shape. What color is it? How big is it? What is it made of?

- How do you want to get rid of it? Be creative. You can even call your favorite cartoon character to help you release it. Give every cell of your body permission to release the memory, the feelings connected to it, the mental patterns attached. Just let it go.

- Are you feeling any emotion? Allow the feelings to bubble up and come out. You are safe to let them go.

- Can you forgive the person or other people involved?

- Can you forgive yourself?

Take a big breath and let it go. Take another breath. When you exhale, allow a sound to come out as it releases.

Fill yourself with light, extending all the way down and out through the soles of your feet and out your fingertips. You deserve love. You are willing to receive from the abundant universe. Abundance is your birthright. You are open to receive all the love and support that you need. It is safe to have what you want. You can have what you want, if it is for the highest good of yourself and everyone everywhere.

End your recording.

Notice the effects. Were you able to forgive? Do you feel different from when you began the meditation? What did you discover? Write down your experience in your journal.

Perfect Scenario

Sometimes we think that circumstances have to be a certain way before we can get what we want. But waiting for the perfect scenario to occur before you take action toward a goal is a trap. If you keep saying, "I'll start dating once I lose five pounds," chances are you will keep postponing dating. And if you do lose five pounds and begin dating but then regain the weight, you'll fall back into a vicious cycle.

Other times, our intentions don't turn out as planned. Many great artists don't become famous until after they've died. Many suffragettes were imprisoned and beaten, and endured hunger strikes before women were granted the right to vote.

But what is most important is that they persisted and didn't give up.

Oftentimes we know what we want, but we don't have a clue as to how to make it happen. We can produce the result by being determined, committed, and willing to change. Some people need a crisis to move them into action, as was the case for Alexandra.

Alexandra's Story

Alexandra and her husband Bob's real estate business kept growing and growing, for the market was booming. The people flocking to the city needed housing. Alexandra and Bob would buy row houses in up-and-coming neighborhoods, rehab them, and then sell them for a profit.

Since Alexandra and Bob were making big money, they kept investing back into the business and taking out loans to buy more properties. They even restored a beautiful Victorian home with hardwood floors and leaded glass windows for themselves in one of the diverse neighborhoods they were rehabilitating. They added a new kitchen with granite counters and a bathroom with a Jacuzzi, making the home a perfect place to raise a family.

Alexandra gave birth to two baby girls over the course of three years. The new parents' entrepreneurial spirit blossomed. Bob invested in a café. Alexandra started a cosmetic business she could run from home while caring for their children. They were a dynamic, happy couple living the American dream. Their good fortune seemed like it would never end— and then the housing market collapsed.

When the real estate market bubble burst, the couple was left with nine properties they couldn't sell. Since property values plummeted, the mortgage on their own home exceeded its value as well. At the same time, overpaid, underhanded management plagued Bob's café. Expenses outweighed income, and vendors who supplied the food and beverages weren't being paid. Bob and Alexandra had bitten off way more than they could chew, and there was nothing to do but ride it out. They were deeply indebted to the bank.

Alexandra and Bob were sure that the real estate market would turn around and the economy would pick up, so they proceeded as if business were as usual. However, since they no longer had income, they began using their credit cards to pay their everyday expenses. Bob tried to get a job as an engineer, his major in college, but he didn't have enough experience to be hired. The bills piled up and seemed to be out of control. They sunk deeper and deeper into debt. Alexandra and Bob were so stressed their lovey-dovey way of relating to each other turned into bickering and arguing. They began fighting over the littlest things.

Pressures at the café needed constant attention, so Bob had no time for family life. Vendors called Bob at all hours of the day and night demanding money. Bob constantly needed to be at the café to straighten out the payroll and deal with employee drama. He was completely consumed by moment-to-moment crises, which in turn ate away at his marriage. Bob also started drinking and smoking heavily to cope. His immune system was so distressed he developed shingles. He was often in an agitated state, exploding at Alexandra and the kids. Alexandra—in her postpartum state—was volatile herself.

The children seemed more demanding and needed more attention. Sasha, the oldest daughter, refused to put on her shoes before going outside. She'd start screaming and kicking her feet. Dressing her to go out took at least twenty minutes. The youngest daughter began wetting the bed.

The love boat they had been cruising on turned into the *Titanic*. Alexandra's cosmetic business brought her an occasional bonus check, but that barely paid the utility bills. She couldn't afford to buy new products or travel to training and sales meetings. Her business was at a standstill, adding more frustration.

Friends would call asking, "How's everything?"

Alexandra was so ashamed of the turn of events in her life, she'd reply, "Things are just fine."

But she wasn't fine. She could hardly cope with not knowing where her next dollar would come from. It was difficult to be bubbly and cheerful while making sales calls as her little girls screamed in the background. She fell into a trap of beating herself up and lost her self-confidence. Bob was so angry and withdrawn; nothing she could say could console him. They barely spoke anymore. Their beautiful home turned into a house of pain. Just being there reminded her of all that had gone wrong.

Alexandra was afraid that if she shared the truth about her circumstances, she'd never be able to rebuild her business. She believed she'd never be able to attract a sales team if people knew she was floundering. In addition, she couldn't face any more loss or rejection, so she continued to pretend that everything was okay. Telling her parents was out of the question because she couldn't bear being judged or criticized. And she was too proud to admit defeat. Being in need of help didn't fit her self-image. She was often referred to as the strong, capable one in her family.

Bob couldn't bear to hear his dad say, "I told you so."

One night while lying in bed, with her husband asleep with his back to her, Alexandra realized she'd reached her limit. She couldn't go on living this way any longer. If things kept going the way they were going, she knew she would drown in the sinking ship. She had too much at stake. What would become of her daughters if she got divorced? She could lose everything: her home, her marriage, her family. And she was not going to let that happen.

The next morning, Alexandra took back her power and reached out to get professional coaching. What she learned from the session was that she needed to face the truth about her situation and begin sharing what was happening to her with her friends and family. To her surprise, when she revealed her real situation, everyone was sympathetic and genuinely concerned. Alexandra's fears lived only in her imagination, not in reality. Support came flooding in with proposals to help. People offered to babysit and buy groceries. Alexandra even discovered an anonymous envelope slipped through her mailbox with a hundred-dollar bill inside. Bob's family helped pay some debts and hired a lawyer who helped them think things through. Alex's mom paid for preschool tuition for the girls, plus she did laundry whenever she came to visit. Pressures began to lighten.

During Alexandra's second coaching call, she realized that her makeup business wasn't growing because she had a limiting belief that no one could do things as well as she could do them herself. She had not been able to build a sales team because she unconsciously believed that people were incompetent and not as motivated as she was. When she changed her belief, she began attracting competent, success-driven people to be part of her sales team. Her income got a perk, but it still wasn't enough.

However, Alexandra had a breakthrough during her next session. She realized that she'd been waiting for someone to rescue her; perhaps this was all a bad dream, and one day she'd wake up and Bob would say that the economy had turned around or that the real estate market was on the way up to where it used to be. But that wasn't going to happen.

The thought hit her like a lightning bolt. "I need to get a job with a steady paycheck." After all, she had a college degree in communications. She'd resisted getting a nine-to-five job because she'd felt trapped when she'd held a full-time job ten years earlier. Back then, her job ate all of her time and energy so that she couldn't build her own business, which was her lifelong dream. But now she knew she had the time management skills to do both.

Alexandra was so determined to find a job that she called friends and asked them for leads, she searched the Internet, and she even perused businesses in town. Two weeks later she was gainfully employed doing marketing for a big company. Having the extra income boosted her attitude, helping her regained her confidence. She used her in-between time wisely to build her cosmetic business.

Having cash flow in helped her marriage enormously. Bob's health improved. Alexandra and Bob began talking about creating the future instead of arguing and rehashing the past. They even took a weekend vacation to restore their romance while Alexandra's mom babysat the children. They sought financial advice as to how to get back on their feet, and an advisor developed a plan for them.

But living in the neighborhood was a constant reminder of failure. The empty houses on their block resembled a ghost town. They loved their house, which they had rehabbed with their own hands and sweat, but it reminded them too much of what had gone wrong. Their babies were birthed here, but that was in the past. They were attached to something that was part of their suffering. They decided to move to the suburbs and start fresh. They didn't know how they would make it happen, but they were determined to do so.

A few months later, they were living in a modern house in the suburbs with a good school system. They had a big backyard with trees and cleaner air. Deer grazed in the yard in the evening. The surrounding houses were populated with friendly neighbors. Alexandra and Bob were back in love again. They had weathered the storm. Money was coming in and debts were being paid. The nightmare was over.

Using the Yamas to Change

Alexandra used the principles of the yamas to get unstuck and take a new course of action. You may want to review them in chapter four and review your notes in your journal to refresh your memory. When Alexandra practiced ahimsa (nonviolence), she stopped beating herself up and began being more kind to herself. She saw the toll the emotional stress was taking on her children and husband, and she could no longer watch them suffer. She saw what she had at stake and became proactive. She reached out for help.

When Alexandra practiced honesty, satya, and told the truth to her friends and family about what was happening, her life began to change. She could no longer try to cover up her circumstances or keep up false appearances. When she stopped pretending things were fine and instead became authentic, she got results.

When Alexandra practiced not-stealing asteya, she realized she was trying to manipulate others to do things for her instead of directly asking for what she needed. She was not allowing people to be themselves. When she gave that up, she attracted powerful, success-driven people who produced results.

Alexandra was attached to her home. She had brought the historic house that had been beaten down by years of neglect back to life. She invested her time, money, and sweat into making it warm and welcoming. The house was beautiful and elegant and had good memories. She didn't want to leave even though the house no longer brought her the same pleasure as it had in the past, when times were good. When she practiced nonpossessiveness, aparigraha, she was able to let go, and became free to move on.

Exercise:
How to Use the Yamas to Change

Go to a clean page in your journal. Write down an area of your life where you feel stuck.

Practice nonviolence, ahimsa, by noting situations regarding this area where you feel anger, jealousy, the need to control, or any other negative emotion. How do you beat yourself up?

- Ask yourself, "Why am I so angry?" or "Why do I feel a loss of power?" Write down your response.

- Are you willing to give up your anger? Are you willing to give up feeling like a victim? Is there a better way you can feel? How can you be more loving? More compassionate? Kinder? What would happen if you responded this way instead?

- Reducing your internal violence by upgrading your emotional reactions can help lessen the hostile responses from others in your situation.

Practice truthfulness, satya, by noting where you are being inauthentic regarding being honest. Where do you try to look good rather than be real?

- What are you afraid will happen if you tell the truth?

- What are you hiding?

- To whom do you need to stop lying?

- When are you going to have the conversation where you come clean?

Practice not stealing, **asteya,** by noticing where you are trying to take what doesn't belong to you regarding your situation.

- Are you exploiting others, or are you allowing others to take advantage of you?
- Are you cheating in any way in this situation? Or are you allowing others to cheat you?
- Do you directly ask for what you want, or try to manipulate an outcome?

Practice moderation, brahmacharya, by noticing if you are honoring pleasure and sensuality in your situation or are going overboard by being hedonistic.

- How are you suppressing yourself?
- Are you creating barriers to intimacy out of fear of being vulnerable?
- Are you overindulging in any way?

Practice nonpossessiveness, aparigraha, by noticing where you are holding on because you're afraid of loss in your situation.

- Where do you feel the holding in your body?
- Can you give up control?
- What would happen if you let go?
- Give yourself permission to trust that the universe will provide you with what you really need.

Aligning with Divine Will Meditation

For this meditation, you'll need an image of the Chariot tarot card from the Rider-Waite deck. If you don't have one, search for the image online. This card has an image of a man riding in a chariot adorned with moons, stars, and other celestial symbols.

This card has deep symbolism. The self is the rider in the chariot of the body. The senses are the sphinxes, and the mind is the reins. This card is a reminder that you are not your mind, body, or personality. The real you is the *self*, or soul. When you surrender to your self and give up trying to control a situation or outcome, matters get resolved with ease.

This meditation can help you connect to your true self. Have your journal and a pen available to write down your insights when you finish.

Place the card before you. Focus on it until you can recall it in your mind's eye. Once you have a sense of what this card looks like, proceed with the following meditation. You may want to record it so that you can be fully in the process.

Begin recording the following script:

Go into a state of relaxation by taking a few deep, connected breaths.

Imagine the Chariot card in your mind's eye growing larger and larger until the figure becomes life-size. Step into the card.

The landscape extends out in all directions. As you look around at your environment, you see a city in the distance. The chariot, two sphinxes, and the driver are in front of you. It is a sight to behold, for they seem to be glowing with light. The charioteer is wearing a suit of armor with crescent moons as epaulets. A belt with the signs of the zodiac adorns his waist, and a crown of stars sits on his head. The radiance of his smile melts away any of your fears or hesitation. He steps out of the chariot and walks toward you, beaming unconditional love. He has a special message for you. Allow it to flow into your awareness. Trust whatever comes—words, feelings, images, or body sensations.

The charioteer invites you to step into the chariot. It is gilded in gold. When you look up at the canopy, you see it is decorated with thousands of stars. When you close your eyes, you see that the stars exist within you. You are part of the entire cosmos. You feel expansive, light, and free. You are a channel of light and love, in tune with the rhythm of the planets. Your life is in divine order, for heavenly forces guide you.

The chariot driver hands you his wand, a symbol of will. Holding it, you align your personal will with divine will. You feel balanced, centered, and focused. You are divinely guided.

You feel confident as you gaze out into the open road that lies in front of you. The road is clear. All you need to do is stay on the road and it will lead you to success, fulfillment, and accomplishment. But the most important thing is that you enjoy the ride. You know what to do. Notice if a scene or vision unfolds on the road ahead. Trust what comes.

You feel empowered and assured. The charioteer smiles and helps you step out of the chariot. As your feet touch the ground, you feel you are back in your body. Thank the charioteer.

Notice what he does or says in reply.

You take one last look around. Step out of the card. When you do, it shrinks back into its normal size.

End your recording.

Write down your experience in your journal.

What was the message from the charioteer?

Did you recognize the charioteer as someone you know?

How did driving the chariot feel? Did you feel in tune with the cosmos? What was your experience?

Did you have a vision about the road ahead? What did the ride into the future look like?

Write down any other insights you had.

Flower Essences that Help You Take Action

Here is a list of essences that will help you get motivated and overcome inertia. Please refer to the Using Flower Essences section in chapter five for dosage information.

- Blackberry helps when one is sluggish and has difficulty taking action to fulfill one's goals. (FES)

- California wild rose aids with accepting the challenges of life that occur when following one's destiny. (FES)

- Cayenne gives a jumpstart to help overcome inertia and break through resistance. (FES)

- Cerrato helps overcome resistance due to self-doubt. (Bach)

- Larch helps overcome paralysis due to fear of failure. (Bach)

- Peppermint relieves mental lethargy. (FES)

- Tansy helps one to overcome lethargy caused by indecisiveness and take decisive action. (FES)

- Walnut helps one gain freedom from the past and set one's path. (Bach)

- Wild oat helps overcome lack of life direction. (Bach)

Record in your journal what essences you choose to take. Take note of how they help you take action. Do you receive any guidance through dreams while taking these essences? Take note of any coincidences or synchronicities that occur. You may want to create an affirmation to say out loud when you take your essence. Note if you have emotions that come to the surface as part of the clearing process. Do you have quick results with this essence? Or do you need to take another essence to get at a deeper issue?

The Forces of Change

Impermanence is the essence of life, and it is composed of three basic forces: creating, sustaining, and destroying. You can see these forces in operation as the seasons change in northern climates. In spring, new life is birthed. Crocuses seem to pop up overnight, and trees begin to sprout leaves. The grass is a fresh, bright green, and the air is sweet. In summer, this process is sustained. Orchards are ripe with fruit, and gardens produce vegetables. In the autumn, plants begin to wither, die, and go to seed, and in winter much of nature is dormant.

These three processes—creating, sustaining, and destroying—are operating in your life all the time. If your life seems out of balance, it could be the result of being overinvested in one process and underdeveloped in another.

For instance, if you are a good shopper, you know how to fill your house with things to make your life comfortable and pleasurable. You are good at creating. However, if you aren't good at sustaining your household items, you may notice that the silverware tarnishes, the moths eat your carpets, or the oven develops a layer of grease and grit. If you don't maintain your car by changing the oil or getting it inspected, it may break down unexpectedly. Or maybe you know how to initiate a relationship, but you don't make the persistent effort to keep it going. Perhaps you don't have the staying power to weather through stormy situations, so you bail out when the going gets rough.

If you are not good at destroying, you may not be able to throw things away. Your house may be cluttered with things you don't need or can't use. Your refrigerator may have foods that have expired, and your drawers are crammed with broken things that never got repaired. You find yourself still wearing your favorite T-shirt from years ago, even though it is faded and has holes. Or maybe you stay in relationships way too long, even though you know you should have left years ago.

Sometimes when forces beyond your control pressure you to change or threaten that changes will be made for you, it is easy to feel victimized and lose your power, as was the case for Ruth.

Ruth's Story

When Ruth called me for a reading, she was distressed about her business and wanted some guidance. Ruth had owned a laundromat in a diverse, multicultural neighborhood in Chicago for the past twelve years. She built the business from the ground up, replacing the old machines left over from the 1950s with new washers and dryers. The place felt comfortable and homey, because she decorated it with paintings by local artists, installed Wi-Fi, and hired friendly college students to launder clothes for the drop-off service. The space was clean and tidy. Parents could bring their children, for there was a small area set aside where they could play. Over the years, Ruth donated money to plant trees on the block, and she always bought tickets to the local Firemen's Ball. She felt she was part of a community. A few years after she bought the laundromat, the business was so profitable and self-sustaining that she started doing graphic design on a freelance basis as well.

But over the past year, Ruth began to see changes in the neighborhood. As the older generation moved out and sold their 1890s homes, a new generation moved in. The houses were rehabbed, and washers and dryers were installed to modernize them; not as many locals needed a laundromat.

The biggest blow came when a competitor moved in around the corner on the main street—a better location for getting foot-traffic customers. For twelve years, Ruth had run the only Laundromat in the area with no competition. The competitor staked out Ruth's business. She stole Ruth's ideas for wash-and-fold specials. She copied her by decorating walls with local artists' art.

"I couldn't sleep at all last night, for I was too worried," Ruth cried into the phone. "This is the first time in twelve years profits were so low. I thought I made a mistake in bookkeeping. If this keeps up, I don't know how I'll be able to pay my employees. I may have to downsize and let a few go. Plus, they're doing construction a block away and have taken away available parking. I'm losing money and don't know what to do," She sobbed.

When I examined her astrology chart, the main theme was change. And if Ruth didn't make changes, changes would be made for her. Ruth felt pressured by outside forces that she couldn't control; she felt victimized. I reminded her that she had a choice and that she was a cocreator in this circumstance.

We looked at her options. If things kept going the way they were going without Ruth doing anything, she would most likely be driven out of business.

"What are other things you could do?" I asked.

"Well, I could go to the upcoming Laundromat conference to get new marketing ideas," she answered. "That's what I did when I first opened. But I feel like I have to start all over again."

"If things stay the same, we get comfortable and we stop growing," I reminded her. "What else could you do?"

"Well, I could see what other people in the area are doing, but I don't want to steal ideas. I could also sell the business and start a new enterprise," she said sadly. I could tell she had an emotional attachment to her Laundromat; it was her baby.

"Do you know what you could do instead?" I probed.

"No, I've never even thought about doing something else. I guess I thought this would go on forever. It never occurred to me that it might not. I guess I was blessed to have it as long as I did."

Ruth promised that she'd explore her options and collect information before she made a choice. Before we hung up, she confirmed she no longer felt powerless and was even entertaining the idea that this change could bring excitement and new beginnings.

When I spoke to Ruth a few months later, she gave me an update. A Laundromat in a different neighborhood burned down, leaving her a new market for customers. She also developed a pick-up and delivery service that helped increase her business.

Exercise:
Turning Points—Discover Your Style

Everyone responds to change differently. Some people embrace the new very quickly, while others may find it hard to release the past and move ahead. This exercise can help you know how you respond to change by looking at how you've responded to events in the past.

You'll need about ten minutes to complete this exercise. Turn to a clean page in your journal and title it "Turning Points." Make a list of major events in your life. Use this list as a guideline, but feel free to add your own events.

- fell in love
- met an important teacher
- bought a car
- moved away from home
- got a tattoo
- discovered a hobby
- changed your appearance
- met a special friend
- went off to college
- took an important workshop or training
- landed your first job
- bought a house
- got married the first time (or second, or third)
- took an important trip

How did these events happen? Were they planned? Did you need a crisis? Did you fall into them?

What happened after you made the choice? Was it different than you expected?

Was the choice made quickly? Were you cautious? Do you need a crisis to change?

Do you jump into new situations without thinking? Did you get involved because it was the thing to do? Did you change because it felt right?

Are you best at creating, sustaining, or destroying? Do you need to develop your ability to create, maintain, or destroy? What are your insights?

Opportunity Knocking Meditation

This meditation can help you get in touch with how open you are to embracing the new and how ready you are to move forward. You may want to record the exercise beforehand.

Begin recording the following script:

Close your eyes and focus on your breath until you are able to feel calm and peaceful. You are centered and relaxed.

Imagine sitting at home in your favorite chair, feeling relaxed and at ease in the early afternoon. All of a sudden, you hear a friendly knock at your door. You wonder, *Who could it be?* as you get out of your chair and go to the door. Imagine that your opportunity is on the other side of the door.

When you open the door, how do you feel? What is your immediate response?

What body sensations are you experiencing?

What thoughts do you have?

Who or what is standing there?

Are you allowing the opportunity to enter with ease?

End your recording.

Write down your responses in your journal.

What insights did you receive?

Is your past experience affecting your present?

Are you fearful of the unknown or excited by it?

Being in Action

Now that you have utilized the tools to clear your resistance to having what you want and have become unstuck, the pace of your life has probably picked up speed. When you are actively engaged in the game of life, excitement replaces boredom. It is easy to swap resignation and cynicism for wonder and enthusiasm. Accepting that change is part of life can make it easier to go with the flow and help you keep your power when circumstances beyond your control challenge you to do things differently. Ultimately, change brings growth and expansion.

Chapter Eight

CHOOSE LOVE

The quality of your life is determined by the quality of your relationships—and ultimately, all your interactions with others are founded on the relationship you have with yourself. The more you know yourself, the easier it is to know what you want and need from others. In this chapter, you will discover what you truly value in a partnership, and the exercises and meditations will help you choose to experience more love and intimacy in each moment.

The Reality about Love

Many people who come to me for an astrology forecast or a tarot reading are wondering if they will ever find true love, since their relationships haven't worked out in the past. They think something is wrong because they live under the false assumption that relationships are supposed to be easy, when, in truth, a relationship is a process that requires continuous effort. People change and grow over time. Relationships need to be cultivated just like anything else; otherwise stagnation sets in.

Most movies and romantic novels support the illusion that if you find the right person, then you'll live happily ever after. But considering our high divorce rate, this isn't always the case.

In a workshop on past-life relationships I attended, led by astrologer Bob Mulligan at the National Council for Geocosmic Research (NCGR) conference, I learned that if you look at the bigger picture from a past-life perspective, most people haven't earned a happy marriage. Most people unconsciously keep repeating their karmic patterns in their marriage, either ones they've internalized from their family or ones from their unresolved past-life scripts. Or they haven't developed enough self-awareness to know their own needs and values or haven't polished their skills in relating to someone else. Relationship is a process.

Our souls are on an evolutionary journey. It takes many human lifetimes to gain enough experience to become enlightened. We mostly become self-aware and learn about ourselves by engaging with others. All relationships can help you grow in some way.

You have attracted everyone in your life for a purpose, beginning with your family members. I know this may be hard for some of you to believe—that you chose your relatives—but using this context can be empowering. The difficult people mirror something in your soul history that must be overcome; they make it so difficult that you are forced to grow in a new way.

For instance, perhaps you have a father who can't control his temper. He flies into a rage at the slightest provocation. He creates drama and upset in social situations; friends are embarrassed to be seen in public with him, and they fall away. Perhaps he breaks the furniture or punches holes in the wall during his tantrums. Family members find themselves the target of blame, so they all loathe being with him. So over the course of a few years, you see the damaging effects of anger that is not expressed in a healthy way. If you are smart and conscious, you become educated in what not to do because you see how destructive this can be. You take a vow and say, "I'll never be like my father." You are motivated to seek out anger-management techniques, and you learn how to channel anger in a healthy way. However, if you are unaware, you go on repeating your father's anger pattern when you raise your own family. Or you keep attracting people who have out-of-control tempers. The karmic pattern keeps being passed down to each generation until someone says, "Enough already," and changes.

Your family relationships set the foundation for the other relationships you develop as you age and mature. They can help you evolve, even though it may be difficult and take effort. Take Sarah's case as an example.

Relationships Begin with You

Sarah came to my office for a tarot reading. She wanted to know if she would ever have a committed relationship. As she shuffled the cards, Sarah said, "I'm thirty-nine years old. It's time to focus on me. I want a committed relationship with a man."

First, for the position representing the heart of the problem, Sarah pulled the Empress card, which suggested that she was the proverbial "Earth Mother." She was soft and feminine and always concerned about other people's needs. With her upbeat personality and generous heart, she was good at being a caretaker to others. The Lovers card, also placed crossing this position, indicated that balance and fairness were key issues for her in relationships.

The Eight of Swords, represented by a woman bound and blindfolded in a fence of swords, was placed in the position of the past or foundation. It seemed to be symbolic of a block.

"I don't have any time to date. I have a full-time job and spend most of my free time helping my two married sisters and my Aunt Claire," she said. "They're the only family I have left. Both of my parents died years ago."

The Six of Cups signified the recent past. The image of a boy and a girl playing together prompted me to ask Sarah if she had children.

"None of my own. Since my sisters live in my neighborhood, I'm their on-call babysitter for my nieces and nephews. It started out by me simply wanting to help out, but throughout the years it automatically became my job. I feel like I can't say no. And I like feeling needed."

The next card Sarah placed on the table was the Queen of Swords, which holds an image of an older woman. "Oh, that's Aunt Claire. She's in her late sixties, retired, and lives two hours away in the Poconos. I visit when I can, but it's a four-hour round-trip drive in the car, if traffic is good. It's hard to get away because I have a full-time job and a house to maintain."

Sarah pulled the Eight of Cups for the position of the probable future. This signified that if Sarah continued to go on this way, she would be left emotionally and psychically drained.

"That's how I feel now," she said with a sigh. "Every two months or so I visit my aunt and sometimes stay overnight. And I always make an effort to drop in on the holidays."

But as Sarah stared at the gloomy figure in the card, she said, "But now when I think about it, my sisters and aunt never visit me. I'm the one who fills up my gas tank and drives to them. I'm always available to take their calls, but if I call any of them, they don't answer unless it's convenient for them to do so. They'd certainly never talk to me if I disrupted a favorite television program."

The next position of the card layout represented the key to her success. When Sarah selected the Death card, she gasped, "Am I going to die?"

"Oh no, that is not the meaning of this card," I said with a comforting smile. "Something has to change here, Sarah."

The final card Sarah placed on the table representing the outcome was the Hermit card.

"If you keep on this path, there is no man in your future; you will keep being a hermit. Maybe a healing session can help you release some old emotional scripts you don't need anymore," I advised.

"I'm ready," she said eagerly, and she scheduled an appointment.

When Sarah returned for her healing session, she filled me in on the latest development.

"Over the last two weeks, I discovered how unhealthy and out of balance my family relationships had become. I'm the one who is always giving but not receiving much in return."

Sarah sat across from me with teary eyes as she told me her story. "I was driving to the Jersey Shore to spend the weekend with a friend who has a beach house there. I can't remember the last time I was able to get away to just relax. When I was an hour outside of town, my cell phone rang. It was my sister telling me that Aunt Claire was in the hospital because her blood pressure had reached dangerous levels, and she was really angry because I hadn't called her all week. I thought, *Why is it my job to always call her? She knows how to dial a phone, yet she never calls me.* But I didn't say that. Instead I said, 'I'll call her.'"

Sarah continued. "When I reached my friend's home, instead of putting on my bathing suit and heading out for a swim, I searched the Internet for the hospital's phone number and called my aunt's room. I expected that Aunt Claire would be happy to hear my voice, so I was surprised when she yelled into the phone, 'You haven't called me all week to see how I'm doing.'

"I couldn't believe she would say that. I've always called her at least once a week to check to see how she's doing. Plus, I was recently at Aunt Claire's house helping get Easter dinner on the table for the family celebration and then spent the night. And before that, when Aunt Claire had knee surgery, I came to the rescue and cared for her dog while she was in the hospital. I stayed and spent the weekend cooking and cleaning while my aunt recovered at home. Her thanks? Telling me, 'You know, you can move into this retirement community when you're forty-five.'

"And to top it off," Sarah's face was bright red as she spoke, "Aunt Claire doesn't listen to the doctor's advice to eat right and go to physical therapy. She breaks her appointments so she can sit on the couch and eat burgers and fries all afternoon while watching soap operas. Instead of being responsible for changing her health habits, she continues eating junk food and doesn't exercise. Now that she has landed in the hospital, she thinks that it my job to take care of her."

Sarah paused to wipe tears from her eyes before she continued. "Something in me snapped. I finally stood up for myself. I answered my aunt's accusation by saying, 'Aunt Claire, I have a full-time job. I have a house to clean and maintain and two cats to take care of. I spend my extra hours babysitting my nieces and nephews. If you don't feel well and want to talk, you can call me. I'm not psychic.'

"When I hung up the phone, I felt relieved. I had stood up for myself. So I had a great weekend on the beach. But on the way home on Sunday night, my other sister called to tell me that angry Aunt Claire has been bad-mouthing me all weekend."

Sarah began to sob as she continued her tale. "Her news ticked me off, but I became livid when my sister had the gall to say, 'You know, it's really selfish of you to go on vacation while she's in the hospital.' Of course, my sisters had no plans of visiting Aunt Claire in the hospital. I felt like my blood was boiling. I told my sister, 'I'm driving, and I can't talk now,' and I hung up the phone."

"I think it's time to do some healing now," I said while helping Sarah onto the massage table.

As Sarah deeply relaxed into a trance state, she declared, "I'm tired of pleasing other people and giving my power away. I feel unappreciated and used. From this moment on, no one will dictate how my life will go. I want a family of my own."

I asked her to imagine reaching through a beaded curtain and grabbing a ball of gold light, placing it into her power center at her navel. When she did, she shrieked, "I MATTER!" She continued to declare in a softer tone, "I choose to stop being a victim. I am powerful."

I continued to give Reiki to Sarah until she appeared to be at peace.

We wrapped up the session with hypnotic suggestions that Sarah loved herself. I could tell that her self-esteem was growing. She was a beautiful person and deserved love. I made her a flower essence of centaury to take at home for the next month, which would help her to stay true to her priorities. When she left my office, she was a new woman.

The last time I talked with Sarah, she had begun focusing on her priorities and was making better choices. She'd joined a dating service and was also seeing a therapist to empower her to make more changes. And she was planning to move into the city, take yoga classes, and attend many social events.

Sarah had set tighter boundaries with her family members and was no longer at their beck and call. She had learned how to say no. In fact, she was beginning to ask others for support.

Your Relationship to You

There's a fine line between helping and enabling. When you *help* someone, you do something for another that the person is not capable of doing. When you *enable* someone, you do something for another that the person could do. Many people who are generous and considerate fall into the karmic pattern of enabling.

Enabling someone may seem like a caring thing to do, but it ultimately hinders growth and development. If you become responsible for someone, chances are you won't hold the person accountable for negative behavior; you will enable the person's bad habits instead. For instance, I once had a client who needed stress therapy because she was exhausted. She had two teenage sons and worked full time as a bookkeeper. Instead of teaching the boys to clean their rooms and cook their own meals, she became their maid. She enabled them to be slobs by spending all of her free time cleaning up the mess they made. She washed the pile of dishes in the sink and took the empty pizza boxes and soda cans out to the trash while they sat on the couch and watched television.

Or in Sarah's case, instead of chastising her aunt for her eating and exercise habits that ultimately led to a health crisis, Sarah took care of Claire when she came home from the hospital.

When you are enabling, there is always a hidden agenda. Manipulation is at the core. Instead of giving and receiving freely, guilt and shame are used to control. Even saying nothing can be enabling a behavior to continue. Perhaps you say nothing out of fear of retaliation or of being physically harmed in some way. Or maybe you are afraid of losing the love of that person. But taking a passive role doesn't help matters.

Focusing on solving other people's problems is a good way to avoid dealing with your own life. For years, Sarah gave too generously of her time to her family because she felt needed. She wasn't ready to devote the time to creating her own family. But when she raised her self-esteem by establishing boundaries and limits to what she would do for others, stopped sacrificing her needs, and took back her power, her life changed in a positive direction.

Exercise:
Checking In with You

Answer the following questions in your journal:

- Do you feel more gratified when you are doing for others rather than when you do for yourself?

- Are you looking to a partner to make you feel worthwhile or happy?

- Are you searching for someone to rescue you from boredom?

- Do you feel guilty when you spend time or money on your own projects?

- Are you always bailing someone out?

- Do you value the approval of others more than valuing yourself?

- Is clear, honest, and open communication missing in your relationships?

- Do you try to solve other people's problems while neglecting your own?

If you answered yes to any of the above questions, use the following exercise to build your self-esteem. If you answered no to the above questions, the following exercise will enhance your well-being.

If you are looking to a partner to make you feel worthwhile, to make you feel happy, to rescue you from a bored or unhappy life, to make you feel complete or whole—well then you have some work to do because these are needs that are never going to be met by anyone other than yourself.

Exercise:
Loving Yourself Checklist

1. Love Your Body

Go to a clean page in your journal and answer the following questions:

- How are you nourishing your physical self on a daily basis? Weekly? Monthly?
- What works?
- What doesn't work?
- What is missing?

Use this list of nourishing activities to supplement your own. Try adding at least one thing from the list as something you will do today. Try adding five to your weekly schedule and at least ten more to your monthly to-do list.

- taking herbal infusions—tinctures that enhance vitality and relaxation
- getting massages or healing treatments on a regular basis
- getting acupuncture at the changing of seasons
- soaking in a Jacuzzi or a salt or aromatherapy bath
- exercising on a regular basis
- eating healthy foods
- resting or taking a nap
- taking a sauna or steam bath
- surrounding yourself with beauty
- getting medical checkups and dental exams
- sleeping enough
- pampering yourself with a manicure, pedicure, haircut, or facial

- wearing beautiful clothes
- breathing clean air

After you have added some of the activities from this list to your calendar, you may discover other ideas to include. Make sure you are doing something nourishing for your body at least once a day. See if you can replace what isn't working in your life with something nourishing. When you are finished scheduling, go to a clean page in your journal and answer the questions that follow in the next section.

2. Love Your Feelings

- How are you nourishing your emotional self on a daily basis? Weekly? Monthly?
- What works?
- What doesn't work?
- What is missing?

Use this list of nourishing activities to supplement your own. Try adding at least one thing from the list as something you will do today. Try adding five to your weekly schedule and at least ten more to your monthly to-do list.

- spending time with a lover, partner, or spouse
- working toward getting in touch with your feelings
- spending quality time with family members
- spending time with friends
- setting aside time for sex or intimacy

- playing and having fun
- putting your house/apartment in order so it pleases you
- spending time with neighbors
- contributing to your community
- playing with pets
- taking flower essences
- enjoying simple pleasures
- giving yourself time to do nothing
- being kind to yourself and others
- cooking for yourself or others
- gardening
- doing charitable acts
- joking and using your sense of humor
- talking and sharing

After you have added some of the activities from this list to your calendar, you may discover you have other ideas to include. Make sure you are doing something nourishing for your emotional well-being at least once a day. See if you can replace what isn't working in your life with something nourishing. When you are finished scheduling, go to a clean page in your journal and answer the questions that follow in the next section.

3. Love Your Spirit

- How are you nourishing your spirit on a daily basis? Weekly? Monthly?

- What works?

- What doesn't work?

- What is missing?

Use this list of nourishing activities to supplement your own. Try adding at least one thing from the list as something you will do today. Try adding five to your weekly schedule and at least ten more to your monthly to-do list.

- spending time in nature

- spending time in prayer or meditation

- playing sports

- showing leadership

- going to church, pagan gatherings, synagogue, or other forms of group worship

- having adventures

- breaking out of your routine

- working toward being in touch with what you want

- taking a break from stress

- traveling

- being creative: dancing, singing, playing music, painting, drawing

- participating in hobbies

- listening to music
- going to art events, dance performances, or plays
- trying something new and different
- collecting things that inspire you
- practicing yoga, martial arts, Reiki, or other spiritual disciplines
- taking on a challenge

After you have added some of the activities from this list to your calendar, you may discover you have other ideas to include. Make sure you are doing something nourishing for your spiritual well-being at least once a day. See if you can replace what isn't working in your life with something nourishing. When you are finished scheduling, go to a clean page in your journal and answer the questions that follow in the next section.

4. Love Your Mind

- How are you nourishing your mind on a daily basis? Weekly? Monthly?
- What works?
- What doesn't work?
- What is missing?

Use this list of nourishing activities to supplement your own. Try adding at least one thing from the list as something you will do today. Try adding five to your weekly schedule and at least ten more to your monthly to-do list.

- reading books that inspire you
- engaging in conversations that are positive, truthful, healing, or empowering
- seeing quality films
- being with people who inspire you
- studying and learning new things
- socializing and meeting new people
- making new friends
- joining groups or organizations
- being informed of local news
- visiting museums
- attending lectures or webinars
- researching material on the Internet
- sharing on social networks
- listening to what others have to say without judging
- communicating and expressing your truth
- writing a blog
- being informed of world affairs

After you have added some of the activities from this list to your calendar, you may discover you have other ideas to include. Make sure you are doing something nourishing for your mental well-being at least once a day. See if you can replace what isn't working in your life with something nourishing.

When you learn to take care of yourself, you can relate to others with freedom and ease. Trouble comes when you look for a partner to satisfy you in ways that you can only fulfill yourself.

Love Straight Talk

While working as a psychic, the most common problem that I've heard over the past thirty years is lack of communication in relationships. People have called, asking me, "Does John want a commitment?" or "Will I be happy with Mary?" Readings can give basic insights to compatibilities, but couples also need to have conversations about their goals and values to avoid major surprises later that could be detrimental to their relationship. Couples with very different interests can have healthy relationships, but those that have conflicting aspirations will have difficulty relating to each other at a certain point. For instance, if you want children and your partner doesn't, you have a major incompatibility. Or if you want monogamy and your partner wants an open marriage, there's bound to be heartache. If your life goals are at opposite ends, the relationship will ultimately become strained to the breaking point.

Everyone has unique interests. The sign of your Venus in your horoscope can provide a clue as to what is important to you. Some people are homebodies who want a partner to share a family life, while others want a mate who will travel and share adventures. Others need intellectual stimulation and want someone that they can talk to, while others want support to climb the ladder of success. But nothing matters quite so much as finding someone who shares your core values because they represent who you are and what you need.

Chemistry is also important, but there has to be a bigger objective outside of sexual attraction in order to make a relationship work. Take Penny's case, for instance.

Penny's Story

Penny came to my office for an astrology reading wearing a low-cut, tight-fitting dress that showed off her voluptuous figure. She was soft spoken and charismatic. At twenty-eight, she was concerned about her two-year on-again, off-again relationship with Tom.

"Does Tom care about me?" she asked. I looked at how their astrology related to each other, and they had very deep karmic ties.

"Just because you have a strong connection doesn't mean he'll make good marriage material," I warned. "You act as though it is all up to him. Wouldn't it be good to have a serious talk with Tom?"

Penny admitted that when they were together, they never discussed anything "real." They never shared their current problems or concerns. Tom wanted to "keep it light." They were always in the moment, joking and flirting, which always led to terrific sex. But after talking with me about it for fifteen minutes, Penny realized she didn't really know anything about Tom's life, except that he worked long hours at an advertising agency. She'd never met his family or spent holidays with him. It was time they had a down-to-earth conversation about their goals.

When Penny returned for a follow-up healing session, I asked how her talk with Tom went. "It was uncomfortable at first. He needed to drink a few glasses of scotch before he opened up. But once he did, it was enlightening. He told me he was in bad financial trouble. His ex-wife took him for every cent. He owes back child support and is in danger of going to jail if he doesn't pay up. He works sixty hours a week, and yet he still can't meet his bills."

I invited Penny to hop up on the massage table. It was covered with a mat that had a crystal grid set in a sacred geometric pattern, which was designed to open energy channels and align *chakras* (energy centers) to improve self-balance. I covered her clothed body with semiprecious stones in a sacred geometric pattern designed to open her energy channels, while meditative music played in the background. She became peaceful as the mandala of amethyst, rose quartz, selenite, apophyllite, lapis, black tourmaline, and citrine helped her to release the stress of the day.

As Penny deeply relaxed into a trance-state, I asked her to scan her body and report anything she noticed.

"I feel a heaviness in my heart," she said softly as tears welled up in her eyes.

"What does it look like?" I asked.

"It looks like a giant yellow ball of wax."

"How much does it weigh?"

"Fifty pounds," she quickly answered.

"Can I place my hands on your heart?" I asked.

"Please do," she said eagerly.

The moment I touched Penny, I began to receive psychic impressions from Penny's past.

"Do you have an Uncle Harry?" I asked.

"Oh God, yes. He always tried to grope me when I was a teenager because I developed early. I wore a 36D size bra when I was fifteen. One time, while I was washing dishes after a family dinner party, Harry came and put his arms around me and pressed his body into mine while I was alone in the kitchen. It was so gross." She began to cry. "But when I told my mother about it later that night, she slapped me across my face. She told me, 'No one will ever want you. You're just a slut.'"

I continued to send Reiki to Penny as she sobbed. After a few minutes, she appeared to be at peace.

"Tell me about the fifty-pound ball of yellow wax," I asked.

"It has turned into a white dove, and it's flying away." She smiled as she shared her revelation.

"Oh my God, all this time I believed my mother—that no one would want me, except for sex. I've never dated anyone who was available. Or I've always had superficial relationships just based on sex because I believed I was unlovable."

"Can you forgive your mother?" I asked.

"Oh, yes. She grew up Catholic and had a lot of hang-ups," Penny sighed.

I placed a Herkimer diamond on Penny's forehead.

"Now that your wise eyes are open, what can you say about your relationship with Tom?"

"Tom's inability to make a commitment has nothing to do with me. All this time, when he wouldn't call I'd think there was something wrong with me. But he has so many financial problems; he's in serious trouble. I don't want that in my life."

She took a deep breath and said, "I need to end it."

I filled Penny's aura with light and gave her hypnotic suggestions that she was lovable and was forming loving relationships.

"How are you feeling?" I asked.

"Peaceful and light," she said with a smile.

She left with the flower essence bleeding heart to help break unhealthy emotional attachments, and buttercup to help her appreciate her special talents.

Exercise: Love Being In Communication

Sharing what you want out of life and what is most important to you can start a dialogue between you and your partner. It is important that you know your partner's goals and values as well, so you can determine if you are compatible.

Answer the following questions on a clean page in your journal.

- What are your values regarding money? Religion? Work? Family? Domestic life? Children? Career? Home? Politics?

- Do you and your partner share common values?

- How important is honesty, integrity, and fidelity to you?

- How important is honesty, integrity, and fidelity to your partner?
- What are your sexual needs?
- Does your partner share your intimacy needs?
- Do you get along with your partner's family?
- How can you become a better communicator?
- Are you a good listener? Would you be able to repeat what your partner says word for word?
- Can you ask your partner questions easily?
- Can you answer your partner's questions easily?
- What areas are uncomfortable for you to discuss? Why?
- Are you able to ask for what you want?
- Are you able to share your goals with your partner?
- Does your partner bring out the best in you?
- Do you feel free to be yourself with your partner?
- Does your partner make you feel safe and secure?
- In what ways do you support your partner? Do you call to check in, give rides, lend money, help with mundane chores, etc.?
- In what ways does your partner support you?

Looking inside yourself can help prepare you for a successful relationship, but eventually you must apply what you've discovered—and that means taking a risk.

You have to trust your feelings and your judgment because it is easy to be seduced by a beautiful or handsome face or sparkling personality. If you base your judgments on only what you see on the surface, it is easy to get hurt when you discover who the person really is inside.

Love Is Tested

All romantic relationships go through different phases. There's the initial stage of getting to know someone. This stage is filled with excitement as you delve into the unknown. The new person can take you on an exhilarating adventure to new places physically, mentally, emotionally, and spiritually. During the first few months of dating, couples are usually starry-eyed and high on the romance. Forget logic—your heart rules over what your head thinks. Even your partner's most irritating habits can be overlooked when hormones are in high gear. He or she seems to be the most charming person in the world, someone who cannot do anything wrong.

But once you begin to build a strong emotional bond, old karmic patterns begin to surface. The initial time frame is different for everybody because it depends on how often you see each other. Eventually the romance starts to fade and reality begins to set in, so your heartthrob may not seem as fascinating. Negative personality aspects begin to emerge. This is the period where you can discover if the person shares your core values. You can also discover if the relationship is worth the effort or the price you'll have to pay to keep it.

The relationship will be tested. You get to see if your partner is there for you when needed most—or if you have a fairweather friend. It's important that your partner walk the talk. The best way to determine if you want the same things from life is to get to know the person over time. Courtney's story is a prime example of this.

Courtney's Story

When Courtney met Mike on an Internet dating site, she had just been laid off from work. She encountered a lot of rejection from potential employers while searching for a new job. Even though she was pretty, qualified, and intelligent, she began to lose confidence. After a few weeks it became hard to apply for new jobs because she felt like no one wanted her. She became depressed.

All of the attention Courtney received from Mike when they began dating cheered her up. He pursued her by calling her and inviting her to a variety of social occasions. Over the next few months, Courtney felt like she was a princess in a fairy tale. Mike was handsome, a sensitive lover, and had good manners. He called her throughout the week to check in with her and paid for their opulent dinners, concerts, and movie tickets. Mike never asked her to choose the movie or the restaurant—he always took charge. Courtney found a job, and she started to feel her life was on an upswing.

After six weeks, over glasses of red wine in a candlelit penthouse restaurant, Mike declared, "I want you to be my girlfriend. I want this relationship to work out. I want to marry you. All the women in my past cheated on me or were mean. You're so nice." The view of the city sparkled as if they were on top of the world.

But after the fourth month of dating, Mike seemed to change. He stopped calling during the week. If Courtney suggested that they do something she wanted to do, Mike always had an excuse—he was too busy working or having a drink with a friend—and he'd suggest that she go alone. Or if she did convince him to accompany her to a social event, he left his good manners at home.

For instance, Courtney loved baseball and was excited when she got tickets to a play-off game. But when Mike arrived to pick her up, he was so hung over from the previous night's drinking binge with "a friend" that his head hurt. He asked her to drive because he could hardly see straight. Courtney was angry, and her intuition said she should break up with him—but she stayed. She told herself that he'd change.

Instead of the situation changing for the better, they spent less time together. And when they did have dinner together, if Courtney would want to talk about politics or even a personal issue she was grappling with, Mike would begin drinking wine in excess and say, "Let's change the subject. This is a nonissue for me." He never cared to discuss what was really important to her. And when he was drunk, he couldn't perform sexually, so that began to put a damper on their romance.

Mike invited Courtney to a cousin's wedding as his date, and he introduced her to his family and friends. But when he started talking to an attractive young woman sitting at their table, he totally ignored Courtney and acted as though she wasn't there. Finally, the busty blonde got up and left. Since Mike didn't introduce the mystery woman, Courtney asked, "Who was that woman you were talking to?"

"Oh, that was Hannah. I've known her since high school. We used to hook up, but it didn't work out. We were roommates for a while. We even traveled to Guatemala together. Don't worry. We're just friends. She's like part of the family, so she's invited to all of our events. We just go out for drinks now and then," he said as he squeezed Courtney's hand.

Two weeks later, Mike invited Courtney to his family's house for Christmas. Courtney sipped champagne out of a fluted goblet and watched as everyone opened their presents in front of the Christmas tree, which was decorated with red glass balls and twinkle lights. Mike added another log to the fire cracking in the fireplace and then sat down next to his brother. Classical music played on the surround sound system. A sprinkling of snow began to dust the ground outside the window. Courtney felt warm and welcome as she tore the wrapping paper off the box from Mike's parents. Inside was a turquoise necklace. It was so beautiful that tears came to her eyes as she said, "Thank you," and fastened it around her neck.

After the presents were opened and another round of champagne was poured, Mike's mom brought out a photo album and sat next to Courtney on the couch. But when Mike's mom made a point of showing photos of Mike and Hannah standing with their arms around each other in front of the Christmas tree from numerous past holiday celebrations, Courtney started feeling uncomfortable. All the family members talked about what a great person Hannah was, as Mike's mom flipped open page after page of pictures of

Hannah and Mike that filled the entire album. The couple posed for Fourth of July picnics, birthday parties, and Memorial Day barbecues.

When Mike's mom said, "She'd be here with us, except her father's ill in Florida, so she went to be with him," Courtney's face flushed with humiliation and confusion. She felt like she was an interloper.

As Courtney walked out the door after the long dinner, Mike's mom said, "We'll see you again … maybe?"

Later that night, after Courtney and Mike returned to his house, Courtney expressed how uncomfortable she'd felt looking at photos of him and Hannah.

Mike said, "You are crazy. Hannah and I are just friends."

"She's your ex-girlfriend. And you've been going out and having drinks with her," Courtney retorted.

"I can't give her up. You just want to control my life," Mike shouted.

"I'm leaving," Courtney said as she walked out, slamming the door behind her.

But Mike called repeatedly the next week, begging Courtney to return.

"I promise I won't see her," he pleaded.

So Courtney returned, and they got back together as a couple.

For a few weeks Mike didn't mention Hannah, and Mike and Courtney were able to rekindle their romance. But after a couple more weeks went by, he began spending week nights working overtime or playing squash. Courtney felt last on the list of important things in Mike's life.

On Valentine's Day, Courtney spent the afternoon cooking a five-course gourmet dinner they'd share by candlelight. She bought Mike a special card with flowery words expressing how special he was and wrote a personal note expressing how happy she was to have him in her life. She wrapped his favorite kind of sweatshirt in handmade paper and tied it with a silk ribbon. Even though the evening cost her a fortune, she felt it was worth it—he was her valentine.

When Mike arrived two hours late with a generic bouquet of flowers from the grocery store, her heart sank.

"I'm sorry, honey, I couldn't leave work. And traffic was really bad," he said as he embraced her.

Courtney tried to be forgiving as she placed the red carnations in a vase and set them on the table. She served the first course and poured a glass of red wine.

"Cheers," she said as their glasses clinked together.

They sat for a moment in strained silence as they ate puff pastry squares filled with wild mushrooms.

Mike looked into Courtney's eyes and said in a monotone voice, "Hannah called today. She has cancer. I have to go see her in the hospital."

Courtney had conflicting emotions. On one level, she felt sorry that Hannah was sick, but she also felt that Mike was playing her as a fool. Once again her dream of being special to someone was shattered, and she was reduced to being number two. Valentine's Day had turned into her worst nightmare.

Courtney's face turned bright red with rage. "You spend less and less time with me, working overtime or playing squash. And now you're going back to seeing her!" she shouted as she stood up from the table.

"You want me to give up playing squash? It's something I love to do! I can't stop working. You just want to boss me around," Mike retorted. He gulped down the rest of his drink and then poured another glass.

"You just see me once a week to get laid," Courtney yelled.

"You have to accept me for who I am. My friends say that it's mean that you want me to stop seeing a friend I've known for fifteen years." He pouted.

"She's more than a friend," she insisted.

"I don't get what you're saying."

"I want more from a relationship. There's nothing more to say but good-bye." Courtney threw his hat and coat at him and yelled, "Get out."

Mike walked out, leaving the filet mignon smoking in the broiler and his presents unopened on the counter.

Love to Learn

When Courtney came in for a healing session, Reiki relieved her grief and loss. Talking about what had happened throughout her relationship helped her see what had worked and what hadn't. She also became clearer on her karmic patterns and core values. When she claimed responsibility for her role in the matter, she understood her mistakes.

"First off, when I began dating Mike, I wasn't in a good headspace. I wasn't having luck getting a new job, and that took a toll on my self-esteem. Mike's attention felt so good, I got romantically involved with him before taking the time to get to know him better. If I had gone slower, I would have seen the warning signs."

"What warning signs?" I asked.

"After six weeks of dating, Mike told me he wanted to make our relationship work. He even said he was interested in marrying me. But after the first four months, he became less and less available. He wasn't willing to make the extra effort.

"When Mike showed up hung over when I invited him to the play-off game, my intuition said he was rude and unable to compromise. He was always in a good mood—as long as we were doing something he chose to do. But when I asked him to do something I wanted to do, he'd be late, not feel well, or be irritable as a way to punish me. He acted passive-aggressive. I didn't listen to my gut feelings that I should dump him. Instead, I gave him a second chance, which made leaving him even harder months later."

"What about Hannah?" I asked. "Was she a red flag too?"

"In that initial meeting at the wedding, he didn't even bother to introduce me. I should have suspected something right then. But I should have said, 'I need to take care of myself. I'm uncomfortable with Hannah. Saying she is just a friend isn't accurate. I love you, but I need to be number one in a relationship.' I was wrong to give him an ultimatum. That only gave him an excuse to say I was controlling."

"What is the main lesson you learned from this?" I asked.

"Instead of stopping the relationship when I recognized Mike wasn't fully available and moving on, I stayed far too long and tried to get him to change. I asked him to do something he couldn't do, and I wound up feeling rejected when he refused. Instead of making myself miserable, I need to be more selective when I date, and I need to learn better communication skills."

Exercise:
Love Is a Great Teacher

Perhaps you've attracted the wrong partners. But if you look at relationships in the context of being responsible for whom you attract, you can see that each relationship experience is truly right for you. Relating to each person provides a stepping-stone to discovering something about yourself and what you need or about how to relate to another person. Each new partner brings one closer to discovering the nature of a true loving partnership. Some people provide hard lessons that take us through the wringer; the lessons learned from some others aren't traumatic at all. And sometimes we learn by default.

Bring to mind a past relationship, and then answer the following questions in your journal:

- What positive qualities did your lover bring out in you?

- What worked and what didn't work in your last relationship?

- Did your partner have the same moral fiber you thought she or he did?

- Was your partner who you thought she or he was?
- How was your judgment off?
- What was your partner's biggest complaint about you?
- Did you stay in the relationship too long? If so, why?
- What made it end?
- What do you need to work on in your own life so that your next relationship has a better chance of succeeding?

Now complete the following activities:

- You may want to get rid of the gifts, letters, or photos that you received from your ex to help you to detach.
- Write a letter thanking your ex for the contribution s/he made to your life. Mail it if it is appropriate. If it isn't, burn it.
- If you notice that you have a pattern around relationships, use the Karmic Pattern Formula from chapter three to clear your unresolved issues.
- If you do yoga, you may want to add simple backbends to your practice to keep your heart open.

What have you learned from this exercise that will help make your next relationship better? It is important to forgive your ex and yourself and stop blaming. Review your responses with your heart and mind open to help you discover what you truly want in a relationship. By knowing what you are looking for and by being able to detect the warning signs to avoid, you can make better choices.

The Lovers Card

In the tarot, the esoteric meaning of the Lovers card is discrimination. Being able to discriminate is an important component of making choices. In astrology, discrimination is a trait of Virgo. But signs are always viewed with their complement, so Virgo is paired with the compassion of Pisces.

Discrimination involves maintaining our separateness, while compassion helps us experience oneness and empathy. We need to develop discriminating compassion to learn how and when and to whom to give. In this way, we keep our well from running dry. Compassion without discrimination leaves us feeling drained and resentful. Discrimination without compassion leads to prejudice and judgments that leave us feeling separate and alone, without emotional satisfaction.

The Rider-Waite Lovers card has an image of a nude man and woman—opposites symbolizing the conscious and unconscious mind. We live in a world of duality, and thereby we are always making choices. The lovers stand beneath an angel, the symbol of the soul or Higher Self. When our conscious and unconscious aligns with Higher Self, we are apt to make choices for our highest good. We are able to attract what we want with ease and velocity. The mountain in the distance is a symbol of attainment and realization. Behind the man is a tree of flames that represents the twelve signs of the zodiac. The tree behind the woman is the tree of the knowledge of good and evil. The serpent coiled around the tree represents *kundalini*, life-force energy.

The Lovers Meditation

This meditation can help you align your subconscious mind, conscious mind, and Higher Self. It will also help you have more love in your life. Have your journal and a pen available to write down your experience when you finish. You'll need the Lovers tarot card from the Rider-Waite deck. If you don't have one, search for the image online.

Place the card before you. Focus on it until you can recall it in your mind's eye. Once you have a sense of what this card looks like, proceed with the following meditation. You may want to record it so that you can be fully in the process.

Begin recording the following script:

Go into a state of relaxation by taking a few deep, connected breaths.

If your mind begins to drift, gently bring your attention back to your breathing.

Imagine the Lovers card in your mind's eye growing larger and larger until the figure becomes life-size. Step into the card.

The landscape extends out in all directions. As you look around at your environment, you feel the warmth of the sun filling you with strength and vitality.

Do you hear any sounds?

Do you notice any smells?

A man is standing on your right. He is part of you; he is your inner male. How does he appear to you? Strong? Weak? Happy?

What does he need from you to feel more balanced?

Allow the response to flow into your awareness. Trust what comes.

You ask, "How can I improve my relationships with men?" Take a moment to listen to the response. Trust what comes into your awareness.

You are drawn to look at the woman on your left. She is part of you; she is your inner female. How does she appear to you? Angry? Confident? Fearful?

What does she need from you to feel more content and secure?

Allow the response to flow into your awareness. Trust what comes.

You ask, "How can I improve my relationships with women?" Take a moment to listen to the response. Trust what comes into your awareness.

You look up at the angel who is resting in a cloud. You can feel the healing energy he radiates filling your heart with a glowing green light. You feel overwhelmed with love.

"I am Raphael, he who heals," he says. "What is it you wish?"

"How can I have more love in my life?" you ask.

The answer may come as a picture, symbol, words, or feelings. Trust what comes.

Take a few more minutes to have a conversation with Raphael and to receive more guidance. You are being told something positive—something for your highest good—that will occur in your near future. This is a message about love. Trust what you see, hear, and feel.

You feel grateful for the guidance you received. You look at the man and the woman. Has their appearance changed at all?

Give thanks for all you received and say good-bye. You feel peaceful and content. Take one last look around. Step out of the card. When you do, it shrinks back to its normal size.

End your recording.

Write down your experience in your journal. What did the environment look like? Did you hear sounds or notice smells? What was the message from the male? Did you recognize him as someone you know? What was the message from the female? Did you recognize her as someone you know? What was the message from angel Raphael? How did it feel? What were you shown?

How does this card meditation feel compared to the Devil card meditation described in chapter two?

Flower Essences that Support Love

Here are a list of essences relating to love and relationships. Please refer to the section Using Flower Essences in chapter five for dosage information.

- Baby blue eyes helps with feeling at ease with oneself. (FES)

- Bleeding heart helps overcome unhealthy emotional attachments. (FES)

- Buttercup aids in accepting the worth of one's life. (FES)

- Centaury develops a strong sense of self. (Bach)

- Chicory helps release possessiveness and dependency. (Bach)

- Holly helps release jealousy. (Bach)

- Larch helps one develop confidence. (Bach)

- Pine releases guilt and self-blame. (Bach)

- Sunflower helps one believe in oneself. (FES)

Record in your journal what essences you choose to take. Take note of how they help you gain love in your life. You may want to create an affirmation to say out loud when you take your essence. Note if you have emotions that come to the surface as part of the clearing process. Do you have quick results with this essence? Or do you need to take another essence to get at a deeper issue?

Love Is Always Present

Now that your self-love has grown, the quality of your relationships has surely improved. Because you know more about what you need and want, you make better choices about with whom you choose to spend your time. You know what is important to you, so you are likely to attract others who share your values. You now have the tools to heal past hurts and be responsible for your choices so that new possibilities for love are opening. Because you are the source of love in your life, you can choose to have love present in every moment.

CHOOSE COMPLETION

I want to acknowledge you for the extraordinary person you are and for being willing to look at your life through a new context. It takes courage to confront painful issues from the past in order to heal and grow. It also takes bravery to risk failure, declare what you want, and go for it.

In reading this book and applying its principles, you've begun an adventure of self-discovery that will bring you unprecedented fulfillment. The more in touch you are with your soul, the more your choices will bring the things for which you yearn: happiness, direction, and purpose. Once you make clearing karmic patterns a priority, you will sense your life taking on more meaning and joy. You can be more fully aware in the present and thereby make better choices on a daily basis.

Using this book as a foundation, you have laid the groundwork to live with integrity. When you live with integrity, your life works with ease. You've reclaimed your power by cultivating your spirituality and becoming accountable for your actions.

Each action you take with gratitude and mindfulness weaves itself into the collective karmic pattern, creating a better world for all.

Now that you've connected to your core values, you know yourself at a new level and are more in touch with what you want. Applying the Karmic Intentions Formula will empower you to create a life of your dreams. But you need to keep practicing what you've learned, for it is easy to slip into old behaviors and bad habits.

It is important to complete the processes you started some time ago when you began reading this book. Use the following questions to reflect on how much you've grown by doing the processes and reading the stories in *Karmic Choices*. Write the answers on a clean page in your journal.

- How has your life changed since you began working with *Karmic Choices*?
- What have you accomplished?
- What were the important breakthroughs?
- What have you learned about yourself?
- What patterns have you transformed?
- What spiritual lessons have you learned?
- How have you restored your integrity?

- What opened up as a result?
- In what areas of your life do you feel you have more power, freedom, and ease?
- How have you become more responsible?
- What flower essences were most helpful?
- In what areas of your life are you now taking action?
- What areas still need work?
- How has your self-love grown through doing the processes in this book?
- Is your lifestyle more in alignment with your values?
- What qualities have you developed as a result of practicing the yamas and niyamas?
- What's next?

Wherever you are in your process is perfect. Some of you have grown in leaps and bounds, while others have taken baby steps. Be patient with yourself. You evolve at your own speed in your own time. Some may need to go back and review healing exercises and meditations to clear a deeper issue. Others' lives may seem to take off like a rocket. Do not judge your life, for everything is in divine order. The processes yield different results and clear different issues each time you use them.

The more you practice the principles in this book, the more mastery you will attain. Remember that growth is cyclic in nature. You have completed a process, and a new beginning is emerging. I'd love to hear all about your breakthroughs, so please feel free to contact me at my website: www.djunaverse.com.

May your karmic choices lead you to happiness and freedom from suffering. I wish you blessings and love.

SUGGESTED READING

A Teacher's Guide for Beginning Yoga, Vijayendra Pratap, PhD, DYP, Sky Foundation, 1991.

Bach Flower Therapy: Theory and Practice, Mechthild Scheffer, Healing Arts Press, 1988.

The Code: Use the Laws of Manifestation to Achieve Your Highest Good, Tony Burroughs, Weiser Books, 2008.

Flower Essence Repertory: A Complete Guide to North American and English Flower Essences for Emotional and Spiritual Well-Being, Patricia Kaminski and Richard Katz, Earth-Spirit, Inc., 2004.

Forgiveness Solution: The Whole-Body Rx for Finding True Happiness, Abundant Love, and Inner Peace, Dr. Philip Friedman, Conari Press, 2010.

Good Life, Good Death: Tibetan Wisdom on Reincarnation, Rimpoche Nawang Gehlek, Riverhead Books, 2001.

The Heart of Yoga: Developing a Personal Practice, T. K. V. Desikachar, Inner Traditions International, 1999.

Here Comes Trouble: Stories from My Life, Michael Moore, Grand Central Publishing, 2011.

Hoodwinked: An Economic Hit Man Reveals Why the World Financial Markets Imploded—and What We Need to Do to Fix It, John Perkins, Broadway Books, New York, 2009.

How to Know God: The Yoga Aphorisms of Patanjali, translated by Swami Prabhavananda and Christopher Isherwood, Vedanta Press, 1981.

Karmic Healing: Clearing Past-Life Blocks to Present-Day Love, Health, and Happiness, Djuna Wojton, Crossing Press, 2006.

The Kybalion: Hermetic Philosophy, Three Initiates, Yogi Publication Society, 1912.

The Law of Attraction, Esther Hicks and Jerry Hicks, Hay House, 2007.

The Legacy of Luna: The Story of a Tree, a Woman and the Struggle to Save the Redwoods, Julia Butterfly Hill, Harper One, 2001.

Light on the Yoga Sutras of Patanjali, BKS Iyengar, Harper Collins, 1993.

Lily Dale Assembly, World's Largest Center for the Science Philosophy and Religion of Spiritualism, has registered mediums that are available year-round. http://www.lilydaleassembly.com/

1001 Pearls of Buddhist Wisdom: Insights on Truth, Peace, and Enlightenment, selected by the Buddhist Society, Duncan Baird Publishers, 2006.

The Secret, Rhonda Byrne, Atria Books/Beyond Words, 2006.

Soul Agreements, Dick Sutphen and Tara Sutphen, Hampton Roads Publishing, 2005.

The Tibetan Book of Living and Dying, Sogyal Rinpoche, HarperSanFrancisco, 1994.

The Yoga Sutras of Patañjali: A New Edition, Translation, and Commentary, Edwin F. Bryant, North Point Press, 2009.

GLOSSARY

Abhinivesha: One of the five kleishas; means "fear of death." When we identify too much with material existence, we stay attached to what is known, and fear the unknown.

Ahimsa: One of the five yamas of Patanjali. Practice nonviolence toward self and others. Be kind and thoughtful, and show consideration to people and things.

Aparigraha: One of the five yamas of Patanjali. Avoid greed. Simplify your life and take only what is necessary.

Arcana: A component part of tarot cards that translates to mean "mystery."

Asanas: Yoga postures that were developed to tone and cleanse the body.

Asmita: One of the five kleishas; the word means "ego." When we identify with our personality or body, we become attached to a false identity.

Asteya: One of the five yamas of Patanjali. Don't steal or take what doesn't belong to you.

Avidya: Means ignorance. It is the root kleisha and main cause of all suffering. When we deny that our true nature is spiritual and divine, we live in ignorance.

Brahmacharya: One of the five yamas of Patanjali. Practice moderation. Be responsible for your sexuality and intimacy needs.

Dharma: Your purpose in the world or mission in life.

Dvesha: One of the five kleishas; means "repulsion." We have an aversion toward things that have produced unpleasant experiences in the past. We fear repeating them because we want to avoid the possible pain occurring again.

Flower Essences: Homeopathic remedies made from flowers that can heal emotional and mental states of duress. British physician Dr. Edward Bach first developed them in the 1930s. Now new remedies from other plant species are available.

Guru: Translates to mean "teacher."

Icaros: Healing songs connected to plant spirit medicine in the shamanic traditions of South America.

Ishvar Pranidhana: One of the five niyamas that means "surrender to the Divine." Develop a relationship with the Higher Power.

Karma: A Sanskrit word that means "action." "What you sow, you will reap."

Karmic Patterns: Repetitive actions we've made in the past combined with automatic choices we make in the present.

Kleishas: States of mind that distort your view of reality that are impediments to spiritual growth.

Law of Attraction: You attract to yourself that which you hold inside you. Like attracts like.

Mala: A set of beads used for keeping count while reciting, chanting, or mentally repeating mantras or prayers.

Mantras: Repetitive Sanskrit words that are a kind of prayer that gives the mind something to focus on.

Maya: The illusion of the material world.

Namaste: Translates to "The divine in me greets the divine in you."

Niyamas: Five basic rules of self-discipline to help you be free from attachments that cause suffering.

Raga: One of the five kleishas; means attachment. When we experience pleasure, we desire to experience it again. When the experience is unavailable, we feel pain.

Rudraksha: A type of seed traditionally used for prayer beads.

Samskaras: Our imprints or conditioning.

Santosh: One of the five niyamas that means "contentment." Be happy with what you have.

Satya: One of the five yamas. Practice truthfulness and honesty with yourself and others.

Saucha: One of the five niyamas that means "purity." Practice cleanliness.

Savasana (Corpse pose): A yoga asana that can help you gradually release your fear of death, for you learn how to detach from your body, thoughts, and emotions.

Shaktipat: An energetic transmission from a spiritual master that awakens the *kundalini*, or life-force energy, of the student. The process dismantles the separation between the ego and one's divine essence.

Soul: The real you is eternal and divine and is connected to everyone and everything in the universe.

Swadhyaya: One of the five niyamas that means "self-study." Know your authentic self.

Tapas: One of the five niyamas that means "austerity." Apply self-discipline.

Tarot: A deck of seventy-eight cards used mainly for fortunetelling, consisting of four suits of fourteen cards, each making up the minor arcana, and twenty-two major arcana or trump cards.

The Yoga Sutras of Patanjali: An ancient sacred text of Indian philosophy.

Yamas: Principles that can help you build an ethical foundation for spiritual development and were designed to purify the mind.

INDEX

A

Abhinivesha, 39, 63, 65, 255

Ahimsa, 111, 112, 195, 196, 255

Aparigraha, 112, 115, 116, 195, 197, 255

Asmita, 38, 48–50, 255

Assumptions, 23, 75, 77, 78, 82, 88, 91, 94

Asteya, 111, 114, 195, 197, 256

Attachment, 39, 51, 139, 205, 257

Automatic Responses, 22, 23, 25

Avidya, 38–41, 44, 48, 107, 256

B

Bach, Dr. Edward, 143, 256

Beginner's Mind, 91, 95

Blame, 41, 76, 211

Brahmacharya, 111, 115, 197, 256

C

Change, 1, 5, 8, 10, 14, 15, 21, 23, 25, 29, 30, 36, 39, 46, 64, 70, 73–75, 77, 91, 95, 103, 104, 107, 111, 122–125, 133, 145, 169, 174, 188, 194–196, 201, 203–208, 210, 213, 233, 234, 240

Core Values, 169, 170, 172, 226, 232, 238, 248

Corpse Pose, 65, 258

D

Devil Card, 45, 46, 245

Dharma, 128, 129, 131, 256

Dvesha, 39, 56, 256

E

Ecstatic dance, 50

Ego, 22, 38, 42, 48, 49, 51, 65, 126, 255, 258

Enabling, 112, 217, 218

F

Feldenkrais, 50

Flower Essences, 143–145, 149, 150, 160, 200, 222, 245, 249, 251, 256

DJUNA WOJTON

KARMIC CHOICES

HOW MAKING THE RIGHT DECISIONS CAN CREATE ENDURING JOY

"Karmic Choices is a must-read for those on the path to self-knowledge, personal change, healing, and inner peace."

—Philip H. Friedman, PhD, licensed psychologist and author of *The Forgiveness Solution*.

Karmic Choices:
How Making the Right Decisions Can Create Enduring Joy.

(Llewellyn 2014)

By Djuna Wojton
www.djunaverse.com

Available in hard copy or e-book at Llewellyn, http://bit.ly/1ayb148

or your preferred on-line retailer.

Karmic Choices:
How Making the Right Decisions Can Create Enduring Joy.
(Llewellyn 2014)

By Djuna Wojton
www.djunaverse.com

Djuna Wojton, BFA, is a spiritual healer, tarot reader, and astrologer with over two decades of experience. She is the director of the Djunaverse Center for Healing Arts in Philadelphia, which helps clients from around the world through classes and private sessions that focus on personal growth. She is the author of *Karmic Choices: How Making the Right Decisions Can Create Enduring Joy* (2014 Llewellyn), and *Karmic Healing: Clearing Past-Life Blocks to Present-Day Love, Health and Happiness*.

By sharing her new perspective on the laws of karma and attraction, Djuna Wojton helps you to fully manifest the life you desire. Discover how you can incorporate a variety of helpful modalities, including yoga sutras, meditation, energy work, and more. When you follow the three steps—clarify, clear, and create— you'll be more satisfied with your life than you ever imagined possible.

I

Integrity, 5, 97–103, 106, 107, 109–111, 116, 134, 230, 231, 248

Intention, 28, 59, 119, 155, 160–166, 173, 174, 179, 180

Ishvar Pranidhana, 130, 256

K

Karma, 2–4, 53, 73, 83, 84, 131, 256

Karmic Patterns, 5, 6, 69, 73, 74, 81, 82, 91, 137, 210, 232, 238, 247, 257

Kleishas, 37–39, 66, 255–257

Kundalini, 42, 242, 258

L

Love, 2, 13, 15, 30, 43, 53, 60, 61, 64, 66, 81, 116, 124, 125, 129, 143, 150, 162, 169, 172, 175–177, 187, 191, 194, 199, 206, 209, 216, 218, 219, 221, 223, 224, 226, 230, 232, 238–240, 243–246, 249–252

M

Moderation, 111, 115, 197, 256

N

Niyamas, 129–131, 150, 249, 256–258

Nonviolence, 5, 111–112, 132, 195–196, 255

P

Point of View, 72, 73, 76, 77, 87, 89

Purpose, 20, 22, 23, 37, 111, 112, 115, 117, 119, 123–130, 140–143, 145, 146, 150, 156, 160, 179, 181, 210, 247, 256

Q

Quick Fix, 31

R

Raga, 39, 51, 56, 257

Reincarnation, 3, 64, 251

Relationships, 2, 6, 26, 58, 64, 69, 74, 76, 77, 81, 97, 99, 101, 103, 104, 115, 167, 171, 172, 183, 202, 209–212, 214, 219, 226, 229, 230, 232, 240, 241, 244–246

Resistance, 51, 85, 142, 174, 181, 184, 200, 208

Responsibility, 8, 19, 21, 25, 41, 71, 73–77, 87, 89, 94, 96, 106, 185, 238

Rolfing, 50

S

Sai Baba, 41–43, 141

Samskaras, 22, 23, 257

Santosh, 130, 133, 134, 150, 257

Saturn, 45

Satya, 111, 113, 195, 196, 257

Saucha, 130–132, 150, 257

Shaktipat, 42, 258

Suffering, 4, 31, 37–39, 51, 67, 92, 130, 135, 138, 157, 167, 194, 250, 256, 257

Support, 2, 8, 14, 19, 20, 25, 30, 95, 119, 123, 124, 132, 143, 149, 150, 163, 165, 166, 180, 187, 192, 210, 217, 226, 228, 231, 245

Swadhyaya, 130, 137, 138, 258

T

Tapas, 130, 135–137, 258

Tarot, 12, 14, 44, 45, 70, 72, 91, 125, 126, 137, 140, 175, 183, 198, 209, 212, 242, 243, 255, 258

The Chariot Tarot Card, 198

The Devil Tarot Card, 44

The Law of Attraction, 151–153, 253

The Lovers Tarot Card, 243

The Magician Tarot Card, 175

The Sun Tarot Card, 125

Treasure Mapping, 160

Truthfulness, 111, 113, 196, 257

V

Vibhutti, 42

Y

Yamas, 110–112, 130, 194, 196, 249, 255–258

Yoga Sutras of Patanjali, 4, 253, 258

Acknowledgments

Thank you to everyone who contributed to this book. I couldn't have written it without you. First I want to acknowledge my clients and those who generously shared their stories, whether they were included or not. It is an honor and privilege to be part of their healing process and transformation.

I am grateful for all of my teachers who have passed their knowledge to me. Thank you to all of my yoga teachers and especially to Dr. Vijayendra Pratap, Rebecca Hooper, and David Newman. Special thanks to my gurus, Shri Brahmananda Saraswati, Sai Baba, Baba Muktananda, and Swami Chidvilasananda. Muchas gracias to the Shipibo shamans for their teachings.

Special thanks to my agent, Diane Gedymin, for her support. I'm grateful for her expertise, commitment, excellence, and guidance. I treasure her sense of humor and continuing faith in me. Her contribution is invaluable.

I'd like to thank everyone at Llewellyn, especially Angela Wix for being my advocate, and Connie Hill, production editor, for her editing expertise.

Thank you to everyone who was involved in the process of writing this book. I give many thanks to those in Janet Falon's writing group who helped in the initial stages of this book. I want to especially thank Janet Falon and Linda George for their helpful comments and technical skills. Thank you to friends, Joseph Eades, Deborah Hoffman, and Maria Fanelli, for reading my drafts with open hearts and minds. They were always there for me, generously giving feedback and encouragement. Thank you to Katherine Haake for her editing wizardry and polishing skills.

I have deep appreciation to those who nurtured me and lent emotional support through the writing process. Thanks to my Reiki group, especially to Steve Sokolow, Gail Curuso, and Aaron Rosenblatt, for their healing light. I am grateful for all of my friends at Landmark Education who have empowered me in seminars and through the communication course team experience. Thanks to Dr. Chenghui Zhu for her relaxing acupuncture treatments and to Monteo Myers for his inspiring hot stone massages.

Most of all, thank you to my husband, Bruce Pollock, for his insights, love, and unconditional support—my best karmic choice.

To Write to the Author

If you wish to contact the author or would like more information about this book, please write to the author in care of Llewellyn Worldwide Ltd. and we will forward your request. Both the author and publisher appreciate hearing from you and learning of your enjoyment of this book and how it has helped you. Llewellyn Worldwide Ltd. cannot guarantee that every letter written to the author can be answered, but all will be forwarded. Please write to:

Djuna Wojton
℅ Llewellyn Worldwide
2143 Wooddale Drive
Woodbury, MN 55125-2989

Please enclose a self-addressed stamped envelope for reply, or $1.00 to cover costs. If outside the U.S.A., enclose an international postal reply coupon.

GET MORE AT LLEWELLYN.COM

Visit us online to browse hundreds of our books and decks, plus sign up to receive our e-newsletters and exclusive online offers.

- Free tarot readings • Spell-a-Day • Moon phases
- Recipes, spells, and tips • Blogs • Encyclopedia
- Author interviews, articles, and upcoming events

GET SOCIAL WITH LLEWELLYN

 **Find us on Facebook**
www.Facebook.com/LlewellynBooks

Follow us on
www.Twitter.com/Llewellynbooks

GET BOOKS AT LLEWELLYN

LLEWELLYN ORDERING INFORMATION

Order online: Visit our website at www.llewellyn.com to select your books and place an order on our secure server.

Order by phone:
- Call toll free within the U.S. at 1-877-NEW-WRLD (1-877-639-9753)
- Call toll free within Canada at 1-866-NEW-WRLD (1-866-639-9753)
- We accept VISA, MasterCard, and American Express

Order by mail:
Send the full price of your order (MN residents add 6.875% sales tax) in U.S. funds, plus postage and handling to: Llewellyn Worldwide, 2143 Wooddale Drive Woodbury, MN 55125-2989

POSTAGE AND HANDLING
STANDARD (U.S. & Canada):
(Please allow 12 business days)
$25.00 and under, add $4.00.
$25.01 and over, FREE SHIPPING.

INTERNATIONAL ORDERS (airmail only):
$16.00 for one book, plus $3.00 for each additional book.

Visit us online for more shipping options.
Prices subject to change.

FREE CATALOG!

To order, call
1-877-
NEW-WRLD
ext. 8236
or visit our
website

Cosmic Karma

Understanding
Your Contract with the Universe

Marguerite Manning

Cosmic Karma

Understanding Your Contract with the Universe
Marguerite Manning

Did you know that before you were born, your soul made a promise with the entire universe to aim higher and do better in this life? Sounds like a tall order! Not to worry, taking care of your contract with the universe is really about taking care of yourself and bringing some balance into your corner of the earth.

Your astrological birth chart reveals your soul's contract with the universe. By connecting the cosmic dots, you can figure out where you came from and the destiny you chose for this life. Fulfilling your contract is just a matter of knowing where to look.

978-0-7387-1054-9, 216 pp., 7 x 7   **$15.95**

To order, call 1-877-NEW-WRLD
Prices subject to change without notice
Order at Llewellyn.com 24 hours a day, 7 days a week!

Blissology

The Art & Science of Happiness

Andy Baggott

Blissology
The Art & Science of Happiness
ANDY BAGGOTT

Become the master of your own life and destiny with a simple four-step process that combines powerful law-of-attraction techniques, cutting-edge science, and the wisdom of some of the world's oldest spiritual traditions. According to author Andy Baggott, we have more control over our life and our feelings than we realize. In *Blissology*, he shows how to reclaim this control and, in doing so, reclaim your power to create the life of your dreams.

This is a real, hands-on approach—you don't need to take great leaps of faith or radically change your beliefs in order to achieve a better life. Simply by using the tools and techniques within these pages, you can immediately begin to understand, practice, live, and share happiness, creating a life that is truly fulfilling and successful.

978-0-7387-2004-3, 216 pp., 5 x 7　　　　　**$14.95**

To order, call 1-877-NEW-WRLD
Prices subject to change without notice
Order at Llewellyn.com 24 hours a day, 7 days a week!

Foreword by James Van Praagh

YOU
ARE THE
ANSWER

Discovering and Fulfilling
Your Soul's Purpose

Michael J Tamura

You Are the Answer
Discovering and Fulfilling Your Soul's Purpose
Michael J Tamura

World-renowned spiritual teacher, healer, and clairvoyant Michael J Tamura shares his wisdom in this inspirational guide to true spiritual empowerment.

Hailed as a "beautiful manual for living" by Echo Bodine, *You Are the Answer* brings us profound spiritual lessons, highlighted by the author's powerful true stories. Discover how to use your intuition, make room for spirit in your life, and respond—instead of react—to everyday experiences. As you build a temple of the soul, you'll learn to recognize truth, create miracles in your own life, and find your purpose for living!

This insightful and moving guide also features a "spiritual toolkit" of daily practices and exercises to help you on your extraordinary journey in consciousness exploration, healing, and spiritual development.

978-0-7387-1196-6, 288 pp., 6 x 9   **$16.95**

To order, call 1-877-NEW-WRLD
Prices subject to change without notice
Order at Llewellyn.com 24 hours a day, 7 days a week!

Includes 6 Steps to Success

Adrian Calabrese, Ph.D.

How to Get Everything You Ever Wanted

Complete Guide to Using Your Psychic Common Sense

How to Get Everything You Ever Wanted

*Complete Guide to Using Your
Psychic Common Sense*

ADRIAN CALABRESE

Love, money, cars, homes, even good health! Learn how you can begin immediately to manifest everything you want or need with the step-by-step approach presented by Dr. Calabrese. Hundreds of her clients and students have achieved outstanding practical results using the methods in this book, which includes an interactive workbook section in each chapter.

978-1-56718-119-7, 288 pp., 7½ x 9⅛　　　　**$16.95**

To order, call 1-877-NEW-WRLD
Prices subject to change without notice
Order at Llewellyn.com 24 hours a day, 7 days a week!

Melissa Alvarez

365 Ways to Raise Your Frequency

Simple Tools to Increase Your Spiritual Energy for Balance, Purpose, and Joy

365 Ways to Raise Your Frequency

Simple Tools to Increase Your Spiritual Energy for Balance, Purpose, and Joy

Melissa Alvarez

The soul's vibrational rate, our spiritual frequency, has a huge impact on our lives. As it increases, so does our capacity to calm the mind, connect with angels and spirit guides, find joy and enlightenment, and achieve what we want in life.

This simple and inspiring guide makes it easy to elevate your spiritual frequency every day. Choose from a variety of ordinary activities, such as singing and cooking. Practice visualization exercises and techniques for reducing negativity, manifesting abundance, tapping into Universal Energy, and connecting with your higher self. Discover how generous actions and a positive attitude can make a difference. You'll also find long-term projects and guidance for boosting your spiritual energy to new heights over a lifetime.

978-0-7387-2740-0, 432 pp., 5 x 7   **$16.95**

To order, call 1-877-NEW-WRLD
Prices subject to change without notice
Order at Llewellyn.com 24 hours a day, 7 days a week!

Daily
Enlightenments
365 Days of Spiritual Reflection

NATHALIE W. HERRMAN

Daily Enlightenments
365 Days of Spiritual Reflection
Nathalie W Herrman

Discover accessible, useful, and spiritual guidance for every day of the year with *Daily Enlightenments*. This easy-to-understand and practical handbook presents a variety of topics, including expressions of gratitude for life, challenging questions about your behavior, and dressing yourself for joy.

Each entry is a simple reminder to improve the quality of your life, and each concludes with a "take away" summary affirmation about how to best apply the spiritual concept to your life. In only five minutes of reading, this practical tool for overall well-being will ground you in a spiritual truth to improve yourself throughout each day. The accessibility and inspiration of this daily reader will bring higher consciousness to the way you do things and ultimately teach you to worry less and pursue your dreams.

978-0-7387-3712-6, 408 pp., 5 x 7   **$17.99**

To order, call 1-877-NEW-WRLD
Prices subject to change without notice
Order at Llewellyn.com 24 hours a day, 7 days a week!

Servet Hasan

Life
in
Transition

An
Intuitive Path
to New Beginnings

Life in Transition
An Intuitive Path to New Beginnings
Servet Hasan

Nobody can escape change, whether it's the loss of a job, home, money, or even a loved one. But when these moments come, you have the opportunity for growth and renewal as swift transition causes you to face so many avoided issues.

Life in Transition is a three-part roadmap for reinventing yourself by uncovering the gifts that emerge from every loss. Through personal stories, practical exercises, meditations, and more, author Servet Hasan teaches you how to embrace your pain with intuition as your guide. In doing so, you'll realize that every challenge represents a lesson that can teach you how to take the next step toward wholeness and reinvent yourself into a stronger person than you were before.

978-0-7387-3833-8, 264 pp., 5³⁄₁₆ x 8 **$15.99**

To order, call 1-877-NEW-WRLD
Prices subject to change without notice
Order at Llewellyn.com 24 hours a day, 7 days a week!

"Through beautifully written vignettes and
simple yet powerful reflections, Sara Wiseman
helps us step into the flow of grace."

—TARA BRACH, PhD, author of
Radical Acceptance

Living a Life of
Gratitude

★ ★ ★

Your Journey to Grace,
Joy & Healing

Sara Wiseman

Living a Life of Gratitude
Your Journey to Grace, Joy & Healing
Sara Wiseman

When you walk through life with gratitude and simply appreciating everything, every single thing, you reconnect with what's truly important in life. The awe and wonder of life is now ever present.

Through 88 illuminating short stories, *Living a Life of Gratitude* will help you slow down, look around, and see your life for what it is. From our first breaths to our last, Sara Wiseman explores the landmarks of human experience: that we are able to be children and have children, that we can learn and love! Even if we have little, we have so much. Read this book, and revel in the beauty of the world.

978-0-7387-3753-9, 384 pp., 5 x 7　　　　　　　**$16.99**

To order, call 1-877-NEW-WRLD
Prices subject to change without notice
Order at Llewellyn.com 24 hours a day, 7 days a week!

Transform Your Life One Room at a Time

MIND
BODY
HOME

TISHA MORRIS

Mind, Body, Home

Transform Your Life One Room at a Time

Tisha Morris

Awaken to the energetic connections between you and your home. When you make conscious changes to your living space, you can transform your life and uncover your soul.

Unlike other books of its kind, *Mind, Body, Home* presents your home as an integral component to holistic living. From foundation to roof, this essential guide correlates every component of your house with its physical, mental, or emotional counterpart in you. Your home becomes a reflection of you, and being more in tune with your home's energy will allow you to make positive changes in your life. Open the door to the heart of your home and discover a whole new way of seeing and living within it!

978-0-7387-3694-5, 264 pp., 6 x 9   **$16.99**

To order, call 1-877-NEW-WRLD
Prices subject to change without notice
Order at Llewellyn.com 24 hours a day, 7 days a week!

THE SERENITY SOLUTION

*How to Use
Quiet Contemplation
to
Solve Life's Problems*

KEITH PARK, PhD

The Serenity Solution

How to Use Quiet Contemplation to Solve Life's Problems

Keith Park PhD

Gain a greater awareness of self, learn how to solve life problems, and achieve the life conditions you desire. By demonstrating how to employ calm focus—an alert yet relaxed, optimal state of mind—*The Serenity Solution* helps you approach situations with an increased range of thinking and improves your ability to see all options when facing difficulties.

This clear and effective guide utilizes the strategies that great thinkers, meditators, and problem solvers have worked with over the centuries to achieve mindful results. Discover a variety of easy-to-follow concepts, simple illustrations, and step-by-step exercises to help broaden insight. Do away with your negative outlook, and bring better health and relationships into full view.

978-0-7387-3678-5, 216 pp., 6 x 9   **$14.99**

To order, call 1-877-NEW-WRLD
Prices subject to change without notice
Order at Llewellyn.com 24 hours a day, 7 days a week!

Garden of Bliss

Cultivating the Inner Landscape
for Self-Discovery

DEBRA MOFFITT

Garden of Bliss
Cultivating the Inner Landscape for Self-Discovery
DEBRA MOFFITT

Garden of Bliss begins on the French Riviera, where Moffitt, despite her glamorous European lifestyle, is unhappy. Realizing that financial success doesn't necessarily equate to happiness, she looks inside herself and decides to make some changes.

The message of her journey is simple: bliss is a destination that exists within all of us. Using the metaphor of a secret garden, Moffitt encourages her readers to manifest this space in the physical world and connect with the divine feminine through nature. *Garden of Bliss* can be read as a stand-alone book or as a companion text to Moffitt's award-winning debut, *Awake in the World.*

978-0-7387-3382-1, 288 pp., 5³⁄₁₆ x 8   **$16.99**

To order, call 1-877-NEW-WRLD
Prices subject to change without notice
Order at Llewellyn.com 24 hours a day, 7 days a week!

Bach Flower Remedies
For Beginners

A Comprehensive Guide to 38 Essences that Heal

DAVID VENNELLS

Bach Flower Remedies for Beginners
38 Essences that Heal from Deep Within
DAVID VENNELLS

The mind and body cannot be separated—what affects one will affect the other. The Bach Flower Remedies contain the subtle vibrational essences of flowers and trees. These remedies correct imbalances in the mental, emotional and spiritual bodies, promoting healing in the physical body.

Every day we are subjected to thousands of distractions, stressors, and pollutants. These myriad influences can wear down our natural defenses and cause frustration, tension, and even physical illness. The 38 Bach Flower Remedies are a safe and natural solution to the challenges of life in the 21st century. The remedies purify and balance the internal energy system, which in turn heals existing health problems—and can even help prevent future problems from manifesting!

Flower remedies are a safe and gentle form of alternative healing. They cannot harm—they only heal. In fact, they can even be given to children, animals, and plants.

978-0-7387-0047-2, 312 pp., 5³⁄₁₆ x 8   **$14.99**

To order, call 1-877-NEW-WRLD
Prices subject to change without notice
Order at Llewellyn.com 24 hours a day, 7 days a week!